Essex*Works.*
For a better quality of life

OR/10 GRE

COL

D0808625

Published by The Reader's Digest Association Limited
London ▪ New York ▪ Sydney ▪ Montreal

The most amazing places to visit in Britain

Contents

Introduction

Britain encompasses an astonishing concentration of natural beauty, rich history, vibrant culture and incredible examples of human inventiveness, folly and fancy. By scouring all parts of the country, the most amazing places – places where you may see or learn something that will make your jaw drop – have been found. Here, you will discover the unexpected – a quirky octagonal house in Devon or a futuristic boat lift in Scotland – or see the familiar cast in a new light – the world's oldest grape vine at Hampton Court Palace or fossilised seashells on the top of Mount Snowdon. Modern wonders include Cornwall's Eden Project and the London Eye – as important in making Britain so fascinating as its more ancient glories, such as the medieval stained glass of Canterbury Cathedral or York Minster.

DIRECTIONS At the bottom of each page are simple directions for finding the places described there. For places such as museums, stately homes or nature reserves, remember to check on opening times before you set out.

The following abbreviations for heritage or conservation organisations are used throughout the book:

EH	English Heritage www.english-heritage.org.uk
NT	National Trust www.nationaltrust.org.uk
Cadw	Welsh Historic Monuments www.cadw.wales.gov.uk
HS	Historic Scotland www.historic-scotland.gov.uk
NTS	National Trust for Scotland www.nts.org.uk
SNH	Scottish Natural Heritage www.snh.org.uk
RSPB	Royal Society for the Protection of Birds www.rspb.org.uk

SOUTHWEST

ENGLAND

Cornwall

DELABOLE SLATE QUARRY Visiting England's oldest working slate quarry is a much quieter affair since miners stopped using dynamite to extract the slate. The quarry, which is now half a mile long, a quarter of a mile wide and 122m (400ft) deep, may have been in use for around 1,000 years. It was definitely operational in the reign of Queen Elizabeth I, when its slate was exported to the Netherlands. Take a tour of the enormous pit, watch 600-tonne slate blocks being sawed and see how the final products are hand crafted.

EDEN PROJECT The domes of the Eden Project bubble from the floor of a disused claypit like an alien life-form. The whole enterprise at Bodelva, near St Blazey, is the idea of Tim Smit – the man behind the Lost Gardens of Heligan – and a triumph of architecture and engineering. A honeycomb latticework of steel supports hundreds of clear hexagonal foil panels, each strong enough to bear the weight of someone standing on it. Inside lies a botanical wonderland.

The vast domes – the biggest is 110m (361ft) across and 55m (180ft) high – are clustered into two groups. The larger cluster, which forms the world's biggest greenhouse, reproduces the Humid Tropics Biome. Here, a waterfall's

DELABOLE SLATE QUARRY ➡ 1 mile S of Delabole off B3314.
EDEN PROJECT ➡ 2½ miles NE of St Austell off A390.

swirling spray hangs in the hot, humid air, and moisture drips from the lush foliage of balsa, mahogany and teak trees, orchids and bamboo. The second cluster is for the Warm Temperate Biome, the environment of regions like the Mediterranean, California and southern Africa – drier and heady with the scent of herbs and orange and lemon trees. The educational centre, known as The Core, has been designed to reflect the principles of plant growth.

GOONHILLY DOWNS Vast white satellite dishes rise from empty heathland, scanning the skies for messages from space. In the distance, the spindly arms of wind generators chop the air. Such endeavour would have seemed pure magic to the people who long ago raised standing stones and buried their dead on Goonhilly Downs.

Goonhilly is the world's largest satellite station. At Future World @ Goonhilly, you can watch – and have a hand in – the tracking of communications satellites able to pinpoint your house from space or follow the movements of galaxies. After that, walk across Goonhilly Downs, a Site of Special Scientific Interest (and the warmest spot in Britain), to find the prehistoric standing stone known as the Dry Tree. The hut circles and round burial mounds of ancient cultures – Bronze Age and Iron Age, spanning some 2,000 years – lie all around among great drifts of Cornish heathers, orchids and lousewort.

GOONHILLY DOWNS ➠ On B3293 between St Keverne and Helston (off A3083 Helston–Lizard road).

POLZEATH BEACH AND THE RUMPS When the
surf is up, wet-suited figures ride the fast waves of rollers
crashing onto Polzeath Beach from the open sea. The South
West Coastal Path leads north from the beach to Iron Age
ditches and ramparts on The Rumps, a craggy promontory
with extensive views over the Camel estuary. The 6-mile
stretch of coast running east from Rumps Point to Port Quin
is spectacular even by north Cornwall's high standards.

ST MICHAEL'S MOUNT The beach at Marazion gives
breathtaking views of St Michael's Mount, with its Tudor
fortress and 14th-century priory church perched at the
summit. Cross the causeway on foot at low tide, or take the
ferry if the sea is up. Then climb through banks of subtropical
trees and exotic flowering plants, warmed by the proximity
of the sea and sheltered in their landward-facing position. At
the top, wander through the castle's armoury, museum and
superbly elegant Blue Drawing Room.

The first church was built after the Archangel Michael was
supposed to have appeared on the island in AD 495. Shortly after
the Norman invasion of England, it was granted to the Abbey
of Mont St Michel in France – the two sites are remarkably
alike. The monks built a priory. Later, Henry VIII made it a
coastal fortress, and in the mid 17th century the St Aubin family
converted the whole place into an extravaganza of a dwelling.

POLZEATH BEACH AND THE RUMPS ➠ Polzeath, 5 miles N
of Wadebridge, signposted from B3314. The Rumps headland,
2 miles N on South West Coastal Path from Polzeath.
ST MICHAEL'S MOUNT ➠ Off Marazion (A394): on foot via
causeway at low tide or ferry (not winter) at high tide.

SOUTHWEST ENGLAND
Devon

A LA RONDE In the late 18th century it was fashionable for the rich to while away a year taking the Grand Tour through Europe. Cousins Jane and Mary Parminter from a wealthy Devon family spent ten years over theirs and returned excited by what they had seen. Inspired by the shape of the octagonal basilica of San Vitale, in Ravenna, Italy, they created A la Ronde (NT). The fantastical structure consists of a central octagon 11m (36ft) high, with two rooms fanning out from each of its eight sides, creating a 16-sided folly. The chief attraction is the Shell Gallery, with a frieze of feathers, seaweed, sand, stones, pottery fragments and seashells – a work so fragile that viewing is by a video link.

BRENTOR CHURCH There's no mistaking St Michael's Church at Brentor – it stands in dramatic silhouette on a granite outcrop, rearing 30m (100ft) above the surrounding fields. The elevated position of the 12th-century church is breathtaking. The path up to the peak can be tricky to find on misty days – rough weather and an ominous atmosphere seem to cling to the tor. Locals recount how a Tavistock curate had to ply labourers with large quantities of whisky before they would agree to build a new track to the church.

A LA RONDE ▶▶ 2 miles N of Exmouth on A376 Exeter road.
BRENTOR CHURCH ▶▶ 1 mile SW of North Brentor, beside minor road – signposted from A386 at Mary Tavy.

14

The elevated position of the 12th-century church is breathtaking

BURGH ISLAND At low water, it is a splashy walk over the sands to rocky Burgh Island. If the tide is high you take the ferry, which doubles as a tractor. An Art Deco seventh heaven awaits in the curves, colour schemes and natural rock swimming pool of the Burgh Island Hotel, built by the millionaire Archibald Nettlefold in 1929. In the bar you can take cocktails where Agatha Christie, Noël Coward and the Duke of Windsor once supped.

CASTLE DROGO Standing on a craggy spur of rock 274m (900ft) above the wooded gorge of the Teign River, Castle Drogo (NT) is the stuff of fairytales. The situation is remarkable, as was the dream of tea magnate Julius Drewe – to build the last great castle in England. He engaged Edwin Lutyens, architect of the Viceroy's House in New Delhi, who realised Drewe's dream in solid granite from 1911 to 1930. Lutyens kept everything simple and allowed the grandeur of the location to speak for itself. The exterior is sombre – a model of restrained good taste, which extends to the interior's plain stone walls and quietly sumptuous furnishings with just a hint of Art Nouveau.

HALLSANDS A few crumbling doorways and walls cling to a rock shelf under the cliffs near the headland of Start Point. Poignant in their ruined state, they are all that remains

BURGH ISLAND ◗▶ Foot crossing at low tide from Bigbury-on-Sea, end of B3392, off A379, 6 miles NW of Kingsbridge. Hotel tractor at high tide.
CASTLE DROGO ◗▶ 14 miles W of Exeter, signposted from A382 and A30.

of the fishing village of Hallsands. It was a decision by distant authority that condemned the settlement. Between 1897 and 1901, half a million tonnes of shingle were dredged from the sea floor here for dock construction work at Keyham, near Plymouth. With its protective shingle bank gone, Hallsands bore the full brunt of the sea. A storm in January 1917 put paid to the village. The fisher families barely escaped with their lives – some had to climb the cliffs in pitch-black darkness to reach safety. No one returned to the ruined houses.

HARTLAND POINT AND QUAY Visit Hartland Point on a stormy winter's day and you experience nature at its most elemental, as huge Atlantic waves burst thunderously up the 100m (328ft) high cliffs. Devon's north coast turns south here, and wind and sea seem to hit the land with double strength. Countless seafarers have been lost and ships destroyed on this 20-mile stretch of shore, dotted with treacherous rocky bays.

Two miles south of the point is the harbour of Hartland Quay, built in a crevice of the cliffs and partly financed by canny West Country adventurers, including Walter Raleigh and Francis Drake. By the 18th century, it was sending out grain, malt and wool, and receiving imports of building materials and fertilisers. The harbour closed to commercial traffic after storm damage in 1893. Today, the old harbourmaster's house is a hotel and a great place to watch the storm waves in comfort.

HALLSANDS ➽ 1½ miles N of Start Point, S of Torcross on A379 Dartmouth–Kingsbridge road.
HARTLAND POINT AND QUAY ➽ Hartland Point, 6 miles W of Clovelly off A39. Hartland Quay, 6 miles W of A39 via Hartland village.

SOUTHWEST ENGLAND
Dorset

BOVINGTON TANK MUSEUM Allow plenty of time for Bovington. A day would not be too long to spend looking at the world's finest collection of armoured fighting vehicles and watching action displays. In all, the museum contains more than 300 exhibits from 28 countries, from veterans of the two world wars to battered Iraqi tanks captured during Operation Desert Storm in the 1991 Gulf War. One exhibit recreates the experiences of a soldier in the trenches of the First World War, when tanks were first used.

CERNE ABBAS GIANT Most chalk hill figures are simple outlines. The Cerne Abbas Giant (NT) is different. Not only does he have a face, nipples and ribs, but he is also shamelessly showing off his manhood. Who he is meant to be – brandishing a great club as well as his virility at all-comers – is a mystery. It is also uncertain how long his 54m (177ft) frame has stood watch on the downland slope above the village from which he takes his name. The best guess is that he represents the Roman demigod Hercules, whose image on coins and statues he resembles. He may date from the 2nd century AD, when the Emperor Commodus, flushed by his conquest of the Scots, added Hercules Romanus to his other titles.

BOVINGTON TANK MUSEUM ▶▶ 2 miles N of Wool off A352 Wareham–Dorchester road.
CERNE ABBAS GIANT ▶▶ ½ mile N of Cerne Abbas off A352 Sherborne road.

CHESIL BEACH For geography students, this narrow spit, backed by the brackish waters of the Fleet, is the classic example of 'longshore drift'. Here, waves, current, backwash and prevailing winds constantly combine to sift and shift the 18 miles of shingle from west to east. The result is extraordinary: stones that gradually increase in size as the bank runs eastwards. Near Bridport, the shingle is known as pea gravel; at Portland, 15 miles away, the pebbles are the size of large potatoes.

GOLDEN CAP If asked to name the highest cliff along the English Channel, most people would probably say Beachy Head. In fact, it is Golden Cap (NT), a 191m (627ft) slumped giant that glows in the low light of dawn and sunset and dominates the wide sweep of Lyme Bay. From the South West Coast Path on the summit, the views extend eastwards to Portland Bill and westwards all the way to Start Point. The rugged heights of Dartmoor can be seen on the western horizon.

This is Britain's Jurassic Park – the sandstone cliffs are stuffed with fossils from the age of the dinosaurs. It was at nearby Lyme Regis in 1811 that 11-year-old Mary Anning found the first fossilised remains of an ichthyosaur – a huge aquatic reptile looking like a cross between a dolphin and a crocodile. Beachcombers are more likely to find the coiled remains of ammonites (prehistoric molluscs), ranging from the size of a 5p coin to that of a car tyre.

SOUTHWEST ENGLAND Dorset

CHESIL BEACH ➡➡ 1 mile W of B3157, between Portland and Abbotsbury.
GOLDEN CAP ➡➡ 1 mile S of A35 Bridport–Lyme Regis road at Chideock.

LULWORTH COVE The almost-landlocked circular cove, scalloped out of towering chalk cliffs, is a scene of breathtaking drama. The finest view is from above, where the footpath curls eastwards towards the Fossil Forest – hollowed stumps of cycads (primitive trees resembling tree ferns) that grew in the age of dinosaurs. The 'forest' lies on the Army's gunnery ranges, so you should not proceed if a red flag is flying. Look out for the Lulworth skipper – a small, moth-like brown butterfly found only along this stretch of coast.

MAIDEN CASTLE The hill-forts that dominate Dorset's downland skylines are the most enduring monuments of Iron Age Britain. Built between the 6th and the 1st centuries BC, they were sophisticated fortresses by the time of the Roman invasion. The only way in was along a winding passage, guarded by timber gates, between ramparts crowned with palisades. At Maiden Castle (EH), the most impressive of the forts, the ramparts and ditches extended for 2 miles around the hill.

In Dorchester's County Museum is the skeleton of a warrior who died defending Maiden Castle, the head of the fatal arrow still lodged in his backbone. The crucial battle took place in AD 43, after the Emperor Claudius ordered the Second Augusta Legion to crush local resistance. At Maiden Castle, the dead, including the museum's unknown warrior, were buried in what could be Britain's earliest war cemetery.

LULWORTH COVE ▶▶ 5 miles S of Wool, via B3071 and B3070.
MAIDEN CASTLE ▶▶ 2 miles SW of Dorchester, off A354 Weymouth road.

SOUTHWEST ENGLAND
Somerset

BATH, ROMAN BATHS Standing in the steamy dimness, watching the steady torrent of hot spring water, it is easy to understand the awe that inspired the Romans to build their baths and temple here in the 1st century AD.

These are the only hot springs in Britain. Every day, for thousands of years, more than a million litres of water at a constant temperature of 46°C have bubbled out of the ground. The early Celts dedicated the springs to their goddess Sulis, to whom the Romans added their own deity, Minerva. Her power is symbolised in the haunting, wild-haired face of the Gorgon that stares down from the re-created temple pediment.

The Great Bath, with its Roman columns, steps and paving, was revealed more than a century ago. Its lead pipes and lining look little different from when they were laid. Close your eyes and you might hear the echo of voices, smell the anointing oil and feel the hot steam. You can even throw a coin, a curse or a prayer into one of the baths, just as the Romans did before you.

CLIFTON SUSPENSION BRIDGE Two huge towered piers, 26m (85ft) high, support the chains that span Avon Gorge's 214m (702ft) breadth. The structure looks delicate, stretched 75m (246ft) above high water, but is strong enough

BATH, ROMAN BATHS ➡ Entrance in Abbey Churchyard.
CLIFTON SUSPENSION BRIDGE ➡ 2 miles W of Bristol city centre, follow signs for Clifton, then Clifton Suspension Bridge.

to carry 4 million cars a year. The chains that curve above it are anchored in solid rock to take the downward force of 162 suspension rods. Far below, the tidal river winds between bare limestone crags on the north side and steep woods on the south. The bridge was designed by Isambard Kingdom Brunel and completed in 1864, five years after his death.

Sadly, it can be a lure for the desperate, and few are as lucky as Sarah Henley whose billowing skirts formed a parachute when she jumped off the bridge in 1885. She landed gently in the river and lived into her seventies.

GLASTONBURY To climb the green cone of Glastonbury Tor is to follow in legendary footsteps. Joseph of Arimathea is supposed to have arrived here from the Holy Land in about AD 60, bringing with him Christianity and the Holy Grail – said to be buried below Chalice Well at the foot of the tor. Legend also says that this is Avalon, the last resting place of King Arthur. By comparison, the 14th-century tower of the Chapel of St Michael, crowning the tor, is a latecomer.

In the town of Glastonbury, Joseph is said to have built England's first Christian church, a wood-and-wattle forerunner of the later abbey. By Saxon times, Glastonbury Abbey was one of the greatest centres of faith and learning in the land. Although in ruins, it still conveys a sense of the power it held over the lives of all around.

GLASTONBURY ➡ 6 miles S of Wells on A39.

SOUTH

ENGLAND

SOUTH ENGLAND
Bedfordshire

SHUTTLEWORTH COLLECTION You can hear the insistent drone of engines overhead, smell the oil and share the excitement of aviation pioneers at Old Warden aerodrome. Displayed in vast hangars are more than 40 lovingly restored aircraft dating from 1909 to 1947. These include a 1910 Bristol Boxkite, a 1919 Sopwith Dove, a 1928 Gipsy Moth, a 1935 Gloster Gladiator, and a Hawker Sea Hurricane and a Supermarine Spitfire, both from 1941.

The man behind the collection – one of the largest in the world – was Richard Shuttleworth, a motor-racing enthusiast and keen aviator. He inherited the Old Warden estate in 1932 but was killed in a flying accident eight years later, at the age of 31. Visitors can watch maintenance and restoration in progress in the workshop hangar, and there are flying displays.

WHIPSNADE TREE CATHEDRAL In a secluded corner of Whipsnade Downs, flanked by wild-flower meadows, is a unique glory: a grass-floored cathedral (NT) made entirely of mature trees and shrubs. Stately avenues of limes delineate the nave. The chancel is a semicircle of silver birch. Horse chestnuts line the north and south transepts, and each chapel is sculpted from a different tree species. A cloister walk of ash

SHUTTLEWORTH COLLECTION ➡ Old Warden Park, signposted from B658, off A1 roundabout NW of Biggleswade.
WHIPSNADE TREE CATHEDRAL ➡ 2 miles S of Dunstable, signposted from B4540 outside Whipsnade village.

trees edges a dew-pond enclosure that collects rainfall. Its four entrance points are marked by pairs of vast cypresses. Shrubs planted here include berberis, cotoneaster, hazel, holly, laurel, privet, may, rhododendron and wild rose.

A visit to Liverpool's Anglican cathedral, while it was still under construction, inspired a local landowner, E.K. Blyth, to create a symbol of faith, hope and renewal after the First World War. Whipsnade Tree Cathedral was planted in 1931–8 in memory of three friends, two of whom had died in 1918.

WILD BRITAIN Yes, this is Bedfordshire, but as you stand enveloped in a cloud of brightly coloured butterflies at what used to be called the Bedford Butterfly Park, you might think yourself in the Amazonian rain forest or the jungles of Malaysia. Among the hundreds of species in the hot, steamy tropical house are the African citrus swallowtail and the zebra, postman and gulf fritillary from South America. The centrepiece of the tropical house – heated to 28°C – is a cascading waterfall, which maintains the humidity the butterflies require.

Wild Britain's other attractions include the caterpillar feeding station and an 'emerging cage', where rows of butterflies hang upside-down to dry their wings before release. A nature trail, leading through 4ha (10 acres) of wild-flower meadows, and a millennium garden, filled with butterfly-attracting plants, let you observe native British species.

WILD BRITAIN ➡➡ Wilden village, 4 miles NE of Bedford, between A421 and B660.

SOUTH ENGLAND
Berkshire

ETON COLLEGE **A sartorial surprise awaits visitors to Eton.** Top hats were doffed for the last time in 1940, but Eton boys still wear black tailcoats dating from around 1850 and pin-striped trousers adopted about 1900. To this school garb the 70 King's Scholars of Henry VI's original foundation of 1440 add an academic gown, and there are blazers for boating, brown jackets for beagling, and fancy waistcoats. Within Eton's walls, a collegiate calm prevails. In the chapel are 15th-century wall paintings found in 1847, three centuries after the college barber whitewashed them over.

QUEEN MARY'S DOLLS' HOUSE **In a single room of Windsor Castle, the world's largest inhabited castle,** stands the smallest of all royal homes – Queen Mary's Dolls' House, a palace in miniature. Designed by the architect Edwin Lutyens at one-twelfth normal size, it was a present for Queen Mary in the 1920s. There is electric light throughout, running water in all five bathrooms, and two working lifts. More than 1,500 craftsmen, artists and writers of the day gave their skills. Some wrote fingernail-sized books for the bookshelves; others painted portraits for the walls. Every item in the linen cupboard is embroidered with a tiny royal monogram.

ETON COLLEGE ➡ N bank of Thames, opposite Windsor.
QUEEN MARY'S DOLLS' HOUSE ➡ Windsor Castle.

ST GEORGE'S HALL AND CHAPEL Look up in St George's Hall and admire the largest oak hammerbeam

roof built in the 20th century – it had to be restored after fire rampaged through Windsor Castle's state apartments in 1992. On the ceiling and walls are the numbered shields of every Knight of the Order of the Garter – note Winston Churchill's at No. 912.

The piers and graceful fan vaulting of St George's Chapel make it one of Britain's most beautiful ecclesiastical buildings. In its choir the brightly coloured banners of every living Knight of the Garter hang over stalls carved in the 15th century.

WALBURY AND INKPEN HILLS Nowadays, walkers climb Walbury Hill for its stunning view across Berkshire,

Hampshire, Oxfordshire and Wiltshire. But people down the centuries have had other motives for clambering to the highest point – 297m (974ft) above sea level – in southern England's chalk downlands. The Celts noted the hill's commanding outlook and built a fort there. Some 2,000 years later, British forces saw that it resembled the location of German coastal batteries in Normandy and used Walbury to rehearse for D-Day.

On nearby Inkpen Hill, public hangings drew crowds until the mid 19th century. A replica of the original gibbet still stands there. Its unusual T-shape meant that two victims could be strung up together, which was what happened to a local villager and his mistress, convicted in 1676 of murdering the villager's wife.

ST GEORGE'S HALL AND CHAPEL ▶ Windsor Castle.
WALBURY AND INKPEN HILLS ▶ 4 miles S of A4, Newbury–Hungerford road.

SOUTH ENGLAND
Buckinghamshire

BEKONSCOT **A working coal mine, a busy fishing port, a place where the trains always run on time,** where windmills grind corn: all these elements of England between the wars are captured in miniature at Bekonscot. The world's oldest model village opened in 1929. It contains miniature lakes, streams, bridges, turreted castles, a zoo, an aerodrome and a caravan park, as well as rows of neat houses, shops and churches.

Farmworkers joyfully harvest the corn, villagers play cricket on the green and model children laugh with delight at the steam fair. The author Enid Blyton was a frequent visitor to Bekonscot, and it includes a replica of her house. More than 3,000 shrubs and conifers, kept to scale using the Bonsai technique, complement the buildings.

IVINGHOE BEACON **Choose a sunny day in early summer for a walk to the top of Ivinghoe Beacon.** The view gradually revealed in the clear air builds anticipation, culminating in a superb panorama from the 230m (755ft) summit. From the expanse of the Bedfordshire plain and the nearby chalk figure of the Whipsnade lion, the eye is drawn southwest to the Chilterns, following the line of the Ridgeway – Britain's oldest road, which starts here and ends

BEKONSCOT ➡ Beaconsfield town centre. Junction 2 off M40, then A40 and A355.
IVINGHOE BEACON ➡ Grassy car park 1½ miles down minor road E of Ivinghoe (signposted to Ivinghoe Beacon) off B489 Dunstable road.

85 miles away, at Avebury in Wiltshire. The beacon's nature reserve is also best in early summer, carpeted with wild flowers and alive with butterflies.

STOWE LANDSCAPE GARDEN Stepping into Stowe (NT) is like taking a trip back to ancient Greece and

Rome, but here temples are set in the grassy vistas of one of England's greatest landscaped gardens. The Grecian Valley and the Temple of Concord and Victory are two of the triumphs of the landscape gardener, Lancelot 'Capability' Brown, who worked here from 1741. He did not start from scratch – other architects and landscape designers, including John Vanbrugh, William Kent and James Gibbs, had worked at Stowe before him.

WADDESDON MANOR Baron Ferdinand de Rothschild was a man who enjoyed spending his money. The results

are to be seen at Waddesdon (NT), the French chateau-style manor he built between 1874 and 1889. An avid collector, the baron filled it with the fruits of 35 years of buying the best that galleries and auction houses had to offer. There is Sèvres and Meissen porcelain, portraits by Gainsborough and Reynolds, Beauvais tapestries and countless pieces of French furniture. In the gardens, a rococo-style aviary houses exotic birds such as kookaburras and Siamese fireback pheasants.

STOWE LANDSCAPE GARDEN ➡ 3 miles NW of Buckingham off A422 Buckingham–Banbury road.
WADDESDON MANOR ➡ 6 miles NW of Aylesbury on A41 Bicester road.

SOUTH ENGLAND
Hampshire

PORTCHESTER CASTLE At high tide, the sea laps against the walls of the amazingly well-preserved, 3rd-century Roman fortress. The walls and most of the bastions survive, with courses of red tiles breaking the grey flint. In the 12th century, Henry I added the keep, on the top of which the names of some of the 10,000 prisoners held at Portchester (EH) during the Napoleonic wars are carved. The Norman church inside the walls, also built by Henry I, is an architectural gem, with bold zigzag moulding and other motifs.

SANDHAM MEMORIAL CHAPEL Making sandwiches in the hospital ward, sorting the laundry, scrubbing the floor, kit inspection – there is something immeasurably moving about the murals painted by Stanley Spencer in Sandham Memorial Chapel (NT) between 1926 and 1932. Nineteen panels detail the minutiae of soldiers' lives without revealing any of the horror, while *The Resurrection of the Soldiers* covers the entire east wall. Spencer served in the First World War in Macedonia. He had already planned a series of paintings depicting the human companionship engendered by war when a Mr and Mrs Behrend decided to build a chapel to house them. Spencer painted the murals, considered by

PORTCHESTER CASTLE ➡ 6 miles N of Portsmouth off A27 Fareham road.
SANDHAM MEMORIAL CHAPEL ➡ Burghclere, off A34, 4 miles S of Newbury.

many to be his greatest work. The chapel was dedicated to Mrs Behrend's brother, Lieutenant H. W. Sandham, who died from an illness contracted in Macedonia.

SPINNAKER TOWER Built on the seabed and designed to represent billowing sails, the 170m (558ft) tower, completed in 2005, draws on Portsmouth's maritime heritage. A high-speed internal lift takes visitors to the three viewing platforms, or you can choose to walk up the 572 steps to the top. Feeling brave? Then stand on the glass floor in the centre of the concrete and steel structure, the largest glass floor in Europe, and look down to the ground underneath. Or step out onto the Crow's Nest viewing platform and feel the wind whistle round you.

WHITCHURCH SILK MILL Shuttles fly from side to side, reeds clunk and clack back and forth. When Whitchurch Silk Mill's 16 power looms are in action, the sound is deafening and the building vibrates. The silk produced includes taffeta and organza in exclusive designs, mainly for theatrical costumes and other short runs of up to 50m (164ft). The red-brick mill, dating from 1800, stands on an island in the River Test. Its waterwheel once powered all the machinery. Nowadays, electricity is used, but on some occasions the big wheel turns to drive the 19th-century winding gear on the top floor.

SOUTH ENGLAND Hampshire

SPINNAKER TOWER ▶ Portsmouth Historic Waterfront.
WHITCHURCH SILK MILL ▶ Winchester Street, Whitchurch, off A34, 10 miles W of Basingstoke.

**WINCHESTER CATHEDRAL From the peaceful Dean
Garnier Garden in The Close,** you will see that the east end of
the cathedral tips dramatically downwards. Today, this is not a
worry, but in 1905 there was a real danger of complete collapse.

The Norman cathedral – at 169m (555ft), Europe's longest
medieval church – is rich in historical associations. In the Middle
Ages, pilgrims gathered here to venerate St Swithun, a
9th-century Bishop of Winchester. William the Conqueror's
son, William II, is buried in the cathedral, and lovers of Jane
Austen will want to see her gravestone in the north aisle. But
by the early 20th century, the whole structure was under
threat. The cathedral had been built on a bog, and its foundations
of beech logs, laid on a gravel bed, were rotting. The high water
table meant that any attempt to remove the logs and underpin
the walls with concrete would be thwarted by water rushing in.

Engineers proposed the use of a diver, and William Walker
was taken on in 1906. First, liquid cement was injected into
cracks in the walls, then trenches were dug under the base of
the walls and allowed to fill with water. Walker, working alone
and in full diving gear, then began filling the trenches with
bags of dry cement, which he slit open so they would absorb
the water. It took him five years to complete the task, a feat
commemorated at the east end of the cathedral with a statue.

Be sure to seek out the crypt, which regularly floods.
When it does, the vaulting is perfectly reflected around Antony
Gormley's contemplative figure, Sound II, standing in the water.

WINCHESTER CATHEDRAL ▶ Winchester city centre.

SOUTH ENGLAND
Hertfordshire

HENRY MOORE FOUNDATION Vast, sinuous sculptures bring an otherworldly feel to a meticulously tended garden and sheep pasture in the countryside at Perry Green, near Bishop's Stortford. They are part of the largest collection of works by Henry Moore, whose organic, semi-abstract forms seem entirely natural in this context.

Moore and his wife Irina moved to Perry Green after their London studio was damaged in the Blitz. They converted two 15th-century cottages into a house, where they spent the rest of their lives, and gradually acquired 28ha (69 acres) of land. The estate includes studios, workshops and barns containing hundreds of Moore's works. The light and airy Sheep Field Barn has three galleries displaying sketches, carvings and sculpture, while sheep graze among the immense and primal pieces set in the surrounding fields. Large Standing Figure: Knife Edge and Three Piece Sculpture: Vertebrae are among more than 30 sculptures that rise out of the gentle landscape.

NATURAL HISTORY MUSEUM AT TRING A polar bear with a mysterious grin greets you – a disturbing encounter, until you notice that almost every exhibit in the Walter Rothschild collection, now part of the Natural

HENRY MOORE FOUNDATION ➡➡ Perry Green, 5 miles SW of Bishop's Stortford, off B1004.
NATURAL HISTORY MUSEUM AT TRING ➡➡ Akeman Street, off High Street, Tring (signposted off A41).

History Museum, is equally lifelike. From the shy okapi, a rare member of the giraffe family, to huge pythons and anacondas, giant turtles and flamboyantly colourful hummingbirds, cassowaries and butterflies, the place is full of eye-popping surprises, with the prize for the most bizarre going to a group of fleas dressed in painstakingly created 'clothes'.

Walter Rothschild was given the land and money for the museum in 1889 as a 21st-birthday present from his father, the financier 1st Lord Rothschild. The young naturalist commissioned the most skilled Victorian taxidermists for his collection of more than 4,000 species – some, such as the dodo and the zebra-like quagga, now extinct – and displayed them in the handsome floor-to-ceiling cases still used today.

SCOTT'S GROTTO Thousands of shells, minerals and smooth flints glimmer and glisten

so that the interior of Scott's Grotto appears to be jewel-encrusted. It is Britain's largest underground folly, extending 20m (66ft) into a hillside in the town of Ware. Its six chambers are linked by passageways and dotted with niches for seating. Beautifully restored, the grotto is one of the surviving elements of the Amwell estate's grand gardens. A Quaker poet, John Scott, laid it out in the mid 18th century and his friend Dr Samuel Johnson described it as 'a fairy hall'. It was saved from destruction in the 1960s, when houses were built all around it.

SCOTT'S GROTTO ➡ Scotts Road, off A119, S of Ware.

Kent

CANTERBURY CATHEDRAL Glowing blue, crimson and vivid green, the 800-year-old stained-glass windows
of Canterbury Cathedral are a visual revelation. High above the stone floor, Adam delves outside the Garden of Eden, the Magi bring their gifts and the murderers of St Thomas Becket burst in on his devotions. These windows were the 'Poor Man's Bible', teaching thousands of illiterate pilgrims about the Bible and the 1170 martyrdom of Becket. In spite of vandalism by Henry VIII's men and later by Puritans, the cathedral has some of the world's best early medieval stained glass. In the Trinity Chapel, the site of Becket's shrine, eight of the 12 windows survive, showing miracles such as a nun being cured of epilepsy.

CHATHAM, HISTORIC DOCKYARD Relive the days of British naval glory in the Historic Dockyard, begun under
Henry VIII in the 1540s, closed down in 1984 and now being restored. In the dry docks stand HMS *Gannet*, a Victorian sloop; HMS *Cavalier*, a Second World War destroyer; and the submarine *Ocelot*, launched at Chatham in 1962. The quarter-mile long Ropery was the longest brick building in Europe when it was constructed in the late 18th century, while the giant roofed slipways are marvels of Victorian cast-iron design.

CANTERBURY CATHEDRAL ➡ Canterbury city centre.
CHATHAM, HISTORIC DOCKYARD ➡ Off Dock Road, Chatham. Access Chatham from M2.

DOVER MUSEUM, BRONZE AGE BOAT The remains of a Bronze Age boat, some 3,500 years old, form the prize exhibit of Dover Museum. Centuries before Moses led the Children of Israel out of Egypt, sailors from Kent were crossing to France in stout seagoing vessels made from oak planks, stitched together with twisted yew withies and waterproofed with moss and wax. Powered by 18 paddlers, boats like this could have carried passengers, goods and even livestock across the Channel. On a calm day, they could have made the crossing in about five hours.

About half the museum's boat has been recovered from the Dover mud. It measures 9.5 x 2.4m (31 x 8ft) and would have been at least 18m (59ft) long. Though blackened by age, it is still easy to make out the withies, wedges and other details of its construction. Also on display is a section of a modern replica boat, made with copies of Bronze Age tools.

HYTHE, ST LEONARD'S CHURCH High on a hill above the seafront boarding houses and narrow streets of Hythe, the parish church of St Leonard's houses one of the strangest sights in any British ecclesiastical building. The crypt is filled with 2,000 human skulls and 8,000 thighbones from people of all ages. The skulls are displayed neatly on racks, and the thighbones are stacked end-on to the wall. They are thought to be at least 1,000 years old and were once believed

DOVER MUSEUM, BRONZE AGE BOAT ➡ Market Square, Dover.
HYTHE, ST LEONARD'S CHURCH ➡ Church Road, Hythe.

to be the bones of battle casualties or plague victims. But it seems more likely that as new graves were dug, earlier bones were removed and stored in the crypt. It is one of only two ossuaries – vaults for holding bones – left in England.

When St Leonard's was built looking out across the Channel from this one-time Cinque Port, it stood on a pilgrims' route. Its huge pillars still have crude crosses and the outlines of medieval ships scratched into their stone. Below the chancel runs a covered passage or ambulatory, built to allow processions to walk right round the church on holy ground. This was later turned into the crypt in which the bones are exhibited.

PENSHURST PLACE Towering 18m (59ft) to its massive chestnut roof timbers, the Baron's Hall in Penshurst

Place is one of England's grandest medieval interiors and the centrepiece of this sprawling mansion of golden-brown stone. The hall was completed in 1341 and is still much as it was six centuries ago, with logs piled in its central fireplace, trestle tables stretching on either side and a floor of well-worn medieval tiles.

In the grounds stands Sidney's Oak, already 500 years old when the house was built. It is named after the Elizabethan hero and poet Sir Philip Sidney, the most famous member of the family that has lived here since 1552.

PENSHURST PLACE ▶ 4 miles W of Tonbridge, in Penshurst village.

Oxfordshire

BLENHEIM PALACE In a country renowned for stately houses, Blenheim is in a class of its own. Even the term 'palace' is inadequate; none of Britain's royal palaces compares in scale – for that you have to travel to Versailles, in many ways the model for Blenheim. Nikolaus Pevsner, the architectural historian, likened it to a titanic piece of sculpture – a good way to regard it. When John Churchill, 1st Duke of Marlborough, won the greatest victory since Agincourt at Blenheim, on the Danube, in 1704, queen and country built a mixture of home and patriotic monument for the national hero. Blenheim was designed by Vanbrugh and Hawksmoor, and eventually cost around £300,000: by the standards of the day, a staggering sum.

KELMSCOTT MANOR A stroll around the gardens of this charming Tudor house on the banks of the Thames soon reveals why they so inspired its most famous resident, William Morris. Every wall and border provides stunning images of foliage and flowers, immediately reminiscent of the wallpaper and textile designs of the leader of the Arts and Crafts Movement. There was something essentially English about the movement, with its nostalgia for a pre-industrial age, and Morris found its perfect evocation at Kelmscott.

BLENHEIM PALACE ➡ 8 miles N of Oxford on A44.
KELMSCOTT MANOR ➡ 2 miles E of Lechlade off A417.

Blenheim eventually cost around £300,000 to build

PITT RIVERS MUSEUM More than 500,000 exhibits are displayed in the huge warehouse-like space of the Pitt Rivers Museum. Prepare yourself for many breathtaking discoveries: from shrunken heads and severed fingers to Hawaiian feather cloaks and a Tahitian mourner's costume collected during Captain Cook's second voyage in 1773-4. General Pitt Rivers, an English soldier and archaeologist, donated his collection to Oxford University in 1884. The handwritten labels and cabinets used for exhibits add to its eccentric charm.

RADCLIFFE SQUARE Nowhere in Britain is so much learning concentrated into such a compact area. The Radcliffe Camera, in the centre of the square, opened as a science and medical library in 1749 and is now a main reading room of the Bodleian Library. Nicholas Hawksmoor drew up an early plan for the domed building, but it was modified and completed by James Gibbs. In 1814, the Allied powers met here for a premature celebration of Napoleon's defeat.

Opposite the Camera is the Divinity School, built in 1483 as a lecture room for theology students. A fan-vaulted ceiling rises over it, with the initials of its patrons carved into 455 roof bosses. Duke Humfrey's Library, above the school, was built to house 300 manuscripts given by Henry V's brother. It is part of the Bodleian Library, the university's research library, which has almost 7 million books on more than 100 miles of shelving.

PITT RIVERS MUSEUM ➡ Oxford city centre. Entrance through Oxford University Museum Natural History (OUMNH) on South Parks Road.
RADCLIFFE SQUARE ➡ Oxford city centre, off Catte Street.

SWALCLIFFE BARN One of the country's finest tithe barns, built between 1401 and 1407 in the village of Swalcliffe, stands as testimony to the skills of medieval carpenters and the durability of English oak. The defining feature of the barn is its roof, supported by nine crucks. Each cruck consists of two massive pieces of timber, cut by a pair of sawyers who split a tree lengthways over a pit with a double-handled saw – one sawyer working on top, the other in the pit. The two lengths of wood were then jointed and pegged to make a giant roof support.

UFFINGTON WHITE HORSE Of all the figures carved on England's chalklands, the Uffington White Horse (NT) may be the most extraordinary. Close up, it is a seemingly random arrangement of bare strips of ground, made by ramming chalk into trenches cut into the turf. From farther away these resolve themselves into the deft strokes of the famous landmark: a wonderfully bold, abstract steed galloping over the escarpment. How the people who carved the figure were able to execute it when they could not stand back and view their efforts is a mystery – as is its exact age. It is known that the Uffington White Horse dates from at least the 1st century BC, because coins from that time are marked with its image, but some experts believe it is older. Its representation on coins offers one explanation of why it was created: as a huge sign advertising the territory of the Iron Age tribe that controlled the area.

SWALCLIFFE BARN ➡ 5 miles W of Banbury on B4035.
UFFINGTON WHITE HORSE ➡ 9 miles E of Swindon off B4507 Wantage–Ashbury road.

Surrey

BROOKLANDS MUSEUM The birthplace of motor racing and aviation captures the fascination with speed. The 1907
concrete circuit banks steeply upwards like a wall of death, and it is easy to imagine the crowds cheering as drivers battled to break the lap record. Nearby is the world's first ticket office for plane passengers: a building the size of a bus shelter.

BROOKWOOD CEMETERY Stone and bronze angels, tall crosses and broken pillars are memorials to Victorian
attitudes to death. In 1852 the London Necropolis Company bought this expanse of heath when the city's graveyards were full. More than 5,000 Commonwealth, US and Allied dead of two world wars lie buried in Brookwood Military Cemetery.

WATTS CHAPEL AND GALLERY The Victorian artist George Frederick Watts spent his last years in the village of
Compton. Dominating the Watts Gallery is a full-size model for his bronze statue Physical Energy in London's Kensington Gardens. In the chapel, his wife Mary created a symbolic Tree of Life. The walls and ceiling are covered in painted plaster decoration – a blend of Art Nouveau and Celtic forms.

BROOKLANDS MUSEUM ⏵⏵ 1½ miles S of Weybridge on B374 to Byfleet.
BROOKWOOD CEMETERY ⏵⏵ S of Brookwood village, 5 miles NW of Guildford off A322 Bagshot road; Military cemetery off A324 Pirbright road.
WATTS CHAPEL AND GALLERY ⏵⏵ 3 miles SW of Guildford off A3.

Sussex

BIGNOR ROMAN VILLA Some of England's finest Roman mosaics lie sheltered on the northern slopes of the South Downs at Bignor. Glowing pictures made up of tiny multi-coloured cubes of stone cover the floors of room after room inside specially built, thatched buildings constructed in Georgian times. The most impressive mosaic shows the head of the goddess Venus. She is flanked by long-tailed birds and fern leaves, and accompanied by winged cupids bizarrely dressed as gladiators. In other rooms, Ganymede is borne aloft by an eagle, a dolphin gambols and a Medusa's head stares out balefully. A 25m (82ft) blue-grey, red and white mosaic runs along the length of one corridor.

The mosaics adorned one of the largest Roman villas found in Britain. Begun in the 2nd century, it lay buried until 1811, when a farmer's plough revealed its splendours.

BRIGHTLING Six follies – an obelisk, an observatory, a cone, a temple, a round tower and a pyramid – surround Brightling. They were created by the village's eccentric squire, John Fuller (1757-1834). The obelisk, Brightling Needle, is visible for miles around. It marks the 196m (643ft) summit of Brightling Down. Close by is the observatory – now a private

BIGNOR ROMAN VILLA ➠ 5 miles SW of Pulborough off A29.
BRIGHTLING ➠ 3 miles S of Burwash off A265.

house – built to satisfy Fuller's interest in astronomy. The 10m (33ft) high Sugar Loaf at Wood's Corner is the result of a wager. A friend challenged Fuller's claim that he could see the church spire of Dallington, the next-door village, from his estate. The friend proved him wrong, so Fuller put up this replica spire within sight of his house at Brightling Park. The temple is in the park, while the round tower lies southeast of Brightling Church. Fuller's mausoleum – an 8m (26ft) high pyramid – was constructed in Brightling churchyard.

Fuller is thought to have planned his follies, which earned him the nickname Mad Jack, to keep local men employed as the Wealden iron industry declined.

CHARLESTON Walls, doors, fireplaces, bookcases, chests, tables, even bedsteads and baths: every imaginable surface at Charleston Farmhouse is covered in paintings by Bloomsbury Group artists who made it their country meeting place for half a century. The painters Vanessa Bell and Duncan Grant moved to Sussex in 1916 and there played host to many of the writers, artists and intellectuals of their time. Visitors included the economist Maynard Keynes and Vanessa's sister, Virginia Woolf. The house has been preserved and partly re-created to appear as it was in the 1950s.

CHARLESTON ▶▶ 7 miles E of Lewes off A27.

RYE

RYE When the original guardians of Rye's 13th-century Ypres Tower kept watch across the Channel for French invaders, waves lapped at the rocks below their feet. Two centuries later, the sea had receded, and the town, renowned for its boat-building, was left stranded 2 miles inland.

For the best vantage point over Rye's higgledy-piggledy red-tiled roofs and cobbled streets, climb the winding steps to the top of the tower of St Mary's Church. A walk around the town reveals half-timbered houses jostling with their Georgian neighbours. The Mermaid Inn has close-set timbers, leaded windows and huge stone fireplaces. Lamb House, named after a former mayor, became the home of novelist Henry James. In the Heritage Centre on Strand Quay, an exquisitely detailed Town Model depicts Rye as it was a century ago.

SHOREHAM AIRPORT

SHOREHAM AIRPORT Few British buildings present a more classic example of Art Deco architecture than the terminal building of Shoreham Airport. Its geometric lines, bold curves, contoured surfaces and bright colours are typical of the design style fashionable when the terminal was built in 1936. It is a welcoming place, with a café where you can watch light planes take off and land on an airstrip that has been in continuous use since 1910. In the Archive and Visitor Centre, next door to the main terminal, you sense what air travel was like in an earlier, more leisurely era.

RYE ▮▸ 11 miles NE of Hastings on A259.
SHOREHAM AIRPORT ▮▸ 1 mile NW of Shoreham-by-Sea between A259 coast road and A27.

SOUTH ENGLAND
Wiltshire

AVEBURY A long tide of history has swept over Avebury (EH/NT) and its surroundings, leaving an extraordinarily fascinating heritage. Part of the village lies within a 5,000-year-old stone circle and earthwork. The Church of St James goes back to Saxon times, and a grand Tudor manor house incorporates fragments of a medieval priory.

Leading southeast from the circle is the Stone Avenue – dozens of pairs of standing stones stretching nearly 2 miles to The Sanctuary, a second ceremonial site. From here, ancient monuments spread out along all points of the compass. Northeast are hundreds of standing stones on Fyfield Down. West lies the West Kennett Long Barrow, a huge Neolithic tomb, and just beyond the A4 – a modern highway paved over a Roman road – is Silbury Hill. Cherhill Down with Oldbury Castle, a 2,500-year-old hill-fort, lies another 3 miles in the same direction. Northwestwards, beyond Avebury, lies the great livestock enclosure of Windmill Hill, constructed nearly 6,000 years ago.

CAEN HILL LOCKS For the crew of a narrowboat, the flight of 16 locks on the edge of Devizes is a daunting prospect. It takes more than two hours to work a vessel through them, opening and closing successive gates to raise or

AVEBURY ➡ 6 miles W of Marlborough off A4 Calne Road.
CAEN HILL LOCKS ➡ 2 miles E of Devizes off A361 Trowbridge road.

lower the water in each lock and convey the craft to the next level. For a bystander, however, the giant watery staircase on the side of the hill is an awe-inspiring sight.

The Kennet & Avon Canal opened in 1810. The challenge facing its engineer, John Rennie, was to raise the waterway 72m (236ft) in the short distance of 2½ miles between the valley of the Avon to the west and the town of Devizes. His solution was to build 29 locks, 16 in close succession up the side of Caen Hill. Each one has a side pond or pound – a reservoir from which the canal is replenished. Photographs in the tearoom at the top of the flight illustrate the restoration of the locks during the 1980s, the last act before the reopening of the canal in 1990.

CROFTON PUMPING STATION A big, riveted red boiler and two magnificent beam engines (a Boulton & Watt of 1812 and a Harvey & Co of Hayle, dated 1846): this is engineering history at its most thrilling, especially at weekends, when it is set in motion – phone for times.

The pumping station lies in the rolling downland countryside southeast of Marlborough. The engineer William Jessop designed it to raise water to the highest point of the Kennet and Avon Canal, a sharp 123m (404ft) above the River Kennet. From here, water could be fed into the locks leading in both directions.

CROFTON PUMPING STATION ▶▶ 6 miles SE of Marlborough off A346 at Burbage.

STONEHENGE In a tantalising game of now you see it, now you don't, the best-known ancient monument in Britain pops into sight, then hides with each crest and dip as you travel east along the A303. Finally, 3 miles west of Amesbury, the road sweeps by almost indecently close. The image of Stonehenge (EH) is so familiar, yet the monument itself retains a capacity to shock when the traveller finally comes face to face with its sheer scale, majesty and aura.

The 4,000-year-old stone circle is just the last phase of a building process going back at least another millennium, to around 3000 BC. To start with there was no stone, just a simple 'henge', consisting of a circular ditch and earth rampart. Within a few centuries a ring of massive timber uprights had appeared inside the rampart, so that it resembled Woodhenge (EH), 2 miles northeast, whose long-eroded timbers are now marked by concrete posts.

Around 2600 BC, the monument began to take on its present form with the replacement of the timbers by about 60 bluestones from the Preseli Mountains in southwest Wales, probably arranged in a double crescent at first, but

much altered since. With each of the stones about 2m (6½ft) in length and weighing 4 tonnes, their transportation and erection show great engineering skill. But the henge is overshadowed by what happened next. During the following three centuries, the real giants arrived: dozens of sarsen, or sandstone, megaliths brought 20 miles from the Marlborough Downs. Thirty of these 25-tonne slabs were arranged in a circle and capped with lintels. Within this, the builders erected five even bigger 'trilithons' – structures composed of two uprights supporting a lintel.

The whole sequence of events reveals growing ambition and technical expertise – a burning desire to build an ever bigger, more permanent structure. The result is not just a stupendous balancing act, but an elegant feat of architecture. Stonhenge's uprights have been shaped so that they taper and the lintels sculpted into curves. The two components are fitted together with rudimentary mortice-and-tenon joints – the shaped top of the uprights slotting into a hole cut on the underside of each lintel. No wonder Stonehenge still stands, instilling awe into the hordes who visit every year.

STONEHENGE ▮▶ 3 miles W of Amesbury off A303.

LONDON

LONDON

BRITISH MUSEUM Known the world over for such wonders as the Elgin Marbles and the Rosetta Stone, the British Museum has become equally famous for a part that few people ever used to see. A £100 million development by the architect Norman Foster, completed in 2000, transformed the Great Court, with its pale Georgian stone walls and imposing side porticos, into Europe's largest covered square. Having remained hidden for 150 years, the courtyard is now enclosed by a soaring glass and steel roof.

Another architectural treasure is the Reading Room, restored to its original 19th-century splendour. Some of the masterminds of revolution, including Trotsky, Lenin and Marx, studied in the huge circular room. Any complaints about communism, the former Russian leader Gorbachev once remarked, should be addressed to the British Museum.

CHELSEA PHYSIC GARDEN Step through a gate in a high brick wall that runs down busy Royal Hospital Road and you find yourself in one of the city's most unusual gardens. Established in 1673 by the Society of Apothecaries on the banks of the Thames – then the only means of access – the Chelsea Physic Garden is the second oldest botanic garden in England after Oxford's. The 1.5ha (3½ acre) green oasis was intended to show early medics how to recognise and use plants

BRITISH MUSEUM ➡ Great Russell Street. Tottenham Court Road/Holborn tubes.
CHELSEA PHYSIC GARDEN ➡ Royal Hospital Road. Sloane Square tube.

60

to cure all manner of ailments. It remains a place of research and education as well as pleasure. Aside from the medicinal plants, the garden includes one of Europe's oldest rock gardens, made from volcanic lava imported from Iceland. A small crop of cannabis grew here until 1982 when a dedicated home botanist jumped over the wall during the night and harvested it.

HAMPTON COURT PALACE
The sheer magnificence and location of this riverside palace – built by Cardinal Wolsey, then coveted and confiscated by his master, Henry VIII – are special enough, but what makes it unique is the way it combines the best of 16th and late 17th-century English architecture. Behind the façades and state apartments that Christopher Wren built for William and Mary in the 1690s, much of the medieval Tudor palace constructed by Wolsey and Henry VIII remains. This includes the Chapel Royal, Great Hall and the Tudor kitchens.

Henry VIII was Hampton Court's most flamboyant royal resident, William III the one who loved it best, but in length of tenure a horticultural occupant upstages them all. The great vine, planted by 'Capability' Brown in 1768, is not only the oldest but – subject to dispute from a cutting planted in Windsor – the biggest in the world, with a 1.8m (6ft) girth and an annual yield of some 230kg (510lb) of grapes. An even more venerable feature of the gardens, the maze, was planted in 1702.

HAMPTON COURT PALACE ➡ Hampton Court station (from Waterloo). Boats from Richmond and Kingston.

HIGHGATE CEMETERY Extravagant statues and ornate Victorian symbols of death – stone urns, lilies, fancy spires and spectral angels – rise proudly from the ground and lurk ominously in the undergrowth of Highgate Cemetery. More than 167,000 people are buried in the 52,000 graves here, the final resting places of Michael Faraday and George Eliot among them. The 15ha (37 acre) site, a 19th-century graveyard for the prosperous classes, has two distinct halves. The east side is better known because it is open to visitors and contains Karl Marx's tomb. The west (only open for guided tours) is overrun by wild flowers, ivy, weeds and brambles. Its impressive Egyptian Avenue, built into a hillside, leads to 36 vaults, with vast iron doors and Egyptian pediments, in the Circle of Lebanon.

KEW GARDENS Seven miles southwest of the capital's centre lies one of Britain's great legacies of empire. The 120ha (300 acres) of flowerbeds, glasshouses and hothouses of the Royal Botanic Gardens, Kew, are largely the creation of Joseph Banks. This eminent botanist, who accompanied James Cook on one of his round-the-world voyages, was president of the Royal Society for over four decades and started the plant collection at Kew. It is now the biggest in the world, with more than 30,000 species. Despite the attractions of the larger Temperate House, a new Treetop Walkway and the Princess of Wales Conservatory, where ten climatic zones

HIGHGATE CEMETERY ➡ Swain's Lane. Archway tube.
KEW GARDENS ➡ Kew Gardens station (from Waterloo) and tube.

share the same roof, the most thrilling structure for many is Decimus Burton's Palm House, completed in 1848. In this masterpiece in cast iron and glass, staircases and walkways lead visitors on a steamy walk among tropical plants.

LONDON EYE Much more than a ride in the sky, the Eye is a major addition to the London skyline, a marriage of art

and technology, with a flavour of the funfair. At 135m (440ft) above the ground, it is one of the capital's tallest structures. A circuit on the continuously moving wheel, aboard one of the 32 futuristic glass-enclosed pods, takes 30 minutes. With views of up to 25 miles all around, it is like being circled by a giant map of the capital and its suburbs. By day, you can play spot the landmark, and on evening rides you will have the thrill of seeing London decked out in all its sparkling finery.

ROYAL OPERA HOUSE The mid 19th-century Royal Opera House was never among Europe's grandest. But

its ambitious restoration and renovation have transformed it into one of the most exciting public spaces in the capital. In addition to the undercover Link walkway between the Piazza and Bow Street, visitors can step inside the cavernous Floral Hall, part of the original Covent Garden flower market, which is now the main bar and congregating area.

LONDON

LONDON EYE ▶▶ Waterloo/Westminster tubes.
ROYAL OPERA HOUSE ▶▶ Bow Street. Covent Garden tube.

ST PAUL'S CATHEDRAL As late as the 1950s, St Paul's reigned magnificently over the capital's skyline, a constant presence with the rest of the city sprawling around its feet. These days Wren's immense 17th-century church tends to announce itself with more of a flourish: appearing suddenly among city high-rises. The dome is its most impressive feature. A pewter tureen from without, ornately painted within, it is one of the largest in the world. The ceiling is a false one, a matter of architectural aesthetics best appreciated from the perspective of the Whispering Gallery. Such are the bizarre acoustics here that a *sotto voce* murmur on one side can, when the church is empty, be heard by someone putting an ear to the wall 30m (100ft) away on the far side of the dome.

SHAKESPEARE'S GLOBE Take yourself back to 16th-century London at the Globe, a reconstruction of the riverside theatre for which Shakespeare wrote many of his plays. Like the original, today's circular, open-air Globe is the work of master craftsmen, using traditional techniques and materials including 6,000 bundles of Norfolk water reed on the roof. Plays, of course, are the thing, staged from April 23 (Shakespeare's birthday) to September. But you can visit the theatre all year. Enter the recording booths to add your voice to prerecorded scenes of his plays and to hear actors read familiar lines – you may be surprised by the many different deliveries of 'To be or not to be'.

ST PAUL'S CATHEDRAL ▶▶ St Paul's Churchyard off
Cheapside. St Paul's tube.
SHAKESPEARE'S GLOBE ▶▶ New Globe Walk, Bankside.
Southwark tube.

SHREE SWAMINARAYAN MANDIR The building popularly known as the Neasden Hindu temple is a labour worthy of the gods – it is also one of love. More than 2,000 tonnes of limestone from Bulgaria, and a similar weight of marble from the quarries of Carrara, in Tuscany, Italy, were shipped to India. There, more than 1,500 volunteer craftsmen chiselled the stone into 26,000 pieces of intricate carving and sculpture. These were then shipped to England, where they were assembled like a giant jigsaw. The whole business took three years to bring to completion. Leave your shoes at the door, step inside and admire gods in their elaborate finery, and visit the exhibition on Hinduism.

SIR JOHN SOANE'S MUSEUM The home of Sir John Soane, the architect of the Bank of England, opened as a museum during his own lifetime ('except in wet and dirty weather') to show his rather eccentric collection of objects. Mainly assembled after the death of his wife in 1815 – some say as a therapeutic means of dealing with his grief – the Aladdin's cave of treasures contains paintings (including works by Canaletto, Reynolds and Turner), architectural models, original Hogarth satirical masterpieces (*A Rake's Progress* and *An Election* among them), a shrine to Shakespeare, Apulian vases and the sarcophagus of Egyptian pharaoh Seti I. There are also timepieces, Napoleonic medals, 325 items of furniture

SHREE SWAMINARAYAN MANDIR ➧ Brentfield Road, off A406 North Circular Road. Neasden tube.
SIR JOHN SOANE'S MUSEUM ➧ 13 Lincoln's Inn Fields off Kingsway. Holborn tube.

(many designed by Soane himself), a model of his wife's tomb and the grave of Fanny, her lapdog. The museum of this remarkable man, the son of a country bricklayer, is unique, highly eclectic and short on breathing space, but it delivers what Soane wanted – an emotional punch.

SMITHFIELD MARKET
While London's other wholesale food markets have been shunted out of the city centre, Smithfield Market is a remarkable survivor. Here, the daily – early morning – business of buying and selling meat still takes place in a triumph of mid-Victorian architecture. The 4ha (10 acre) cast-iron structure – much embellished and now fully restored – is fancy enough to hang works of art in, let alone sides of beef, lamb or venison.

Meat has been traded on the site for more than 800 years – the livestock was once slaughtered on the spot. The space was also used for jousting, horse sales, executions and St Bartholomew's Fair, named after the nearby church of St Bartholomew the Great – London's oldest and one of the few survivors of medieval times. More than just a market, Smithfield today stands at the hub of a fashionable part of town, especially on the northern side, where a number of smart restaurants have sprouted up. This is also the place for pubs that are open in the small hours of the morning, and cafés that serve cholesterol-laden breakfasts.

SMITHFIELD MARKET ▶▶ Charterhouse Street off Farringdon Road. Farringdon/Barbican tubes.

TATE MODERN A gentle slope leads you into the depths of a former power station on the banks of the River Thames.

The Bankside station, built by the architect Sir Giles Gilbert Scott between 1947 and 1963, has been transformed into the Tate Modern, a £134 million showcase for the part of the Tate's collection that dates from 1900 to the present day. After it opened in 2000, it quickly became one of Britain's three leading visitor attractions, with more than 5 million visitors in its first year alone.

As you enter the immense space of the Turbine Hall, its interior engulfs you like a whale swallowing plankton. Tall, cathedral-like windows illuminate the bolted pillars and industrial lifts inside and the hum of the transformer station – still operating on the building's south side – creates a quiet background chant. The effect of the space is every bit as thrilling as that of the works of art by Picasso, Matisse, Rothko, Dali, Warhol, Pollock, Giacometti and countless other modern masters.

WESTMINSTER ABBEY Nowhere else can you stand in the presence of the mortal remains of so many major

players in English history and literature. Besides the graves of poets, dramatists and novelists – including Chaucer, Ben Jonson (buried upright in the nave), Samuel Johnson, Charles Dickens, Tennyson, Rudyard Kipling and Thomas Hardy –

TATE MODERN ▶▶ Bankside. Southwark tube.
WESTMINSTER ABBEY ▶▶ Westminster tube.

burial space is heavily populated by kings and queens, from Edward the Confessor, who founded the abbey in 1065, to George II, the last monarch to be interred here in 1760.

The body of the saintly Edward lies at the heart of the abbey, in a magnificent tomb behind the High Altar. But continue past it into an even more glorious shrine to absolute power – Henry VII's Lady Chapel. Go through the fine bronze gates, displaying the Royal Tudor badges, and gasp at the intricacy of the vaulted roof soaring high above. Authority still radiates from the marble effigies, particularly from that of perhaps the greatest of England's rulers, Elizabeth I.

WETLAND CENTRE Europe's largest wetland-creation project

is built on the site of four redundant reservoirs. Five years in the making, the mosaic of lagoons, lakes, ponds and pools, which opened in May 2000, covers just over 40ha (100 acres). Fourteen habitats, from Australian billabong to Siberian tundra, have been created in the outdoor exhibition areas, and some 140 species of birds recorded – as many as 70 in one day, including the kingfisher, and, in 2002, a bittern. The observatory in the Peter Scott Visitor Centre lets you birdwatch in comfort.

WETLAND CENTRE ➽ Queen Elizabeth's Walk, Barnes, off A306. Hammersmith tube (then 'Duck Bus').

EAST ANGLIA

Cambridgeshire

DUXFORD, IMPERIAL WAR MUSEUM All the classic aeroplanes of an enthusiast's dreams are here

in this 180-aircraft collection. Wander from Spitfire to Lancaster, from First World War stringbags such as the Bristol Fighter to big delta-winged Vulcan bombers of the Cold War era, from Mustang fighters of the Second World War to a sinister B-52 bomber that pounded the jungles of Vietnam.

The cream of the American collection is displayed in one of Britain's boldest modern buildings, a glass-walled hangar 18m (59ft) tall, designed by Norman Foster. It has been dedicated as a memorial to the 30,000 US airmen who died while flying wartime missions from Britain – many from Duxford.

ELY CATHEDRAL, OCTAGON TOWER AND LANTERN Sailing the flat fenland barley fields like a stately ship,

the great Octagon Tower of Ely Cathedral, topped by a huge wooden lantern, is an unforgettable sight. Nothing in Britain compares with this wonder of medieval engineering. The Octagon – 22m (72ft) in diameter and weighing 400 tonnes – was created in 1322-8 by a monk, Alan de Walsingham, to replace a collapsed Norman tower. It then took William Hurley, Edward III's master carpenter, 14 years to build the lantern.

DUXFORD, IMPERIAL WAR MUSEUM ➡ 8 miles S of Cambridge on A505.
ELY CATHEDRAL, OCTAGON TOWER AND LANTERN ➡ Ely city centre. Off A10/A142.

FITZWILLIAM MUSEUM A wandering policy is best here, letting the Fitzwilliam's huge number of treasures surprise and delight. Exquisite Ming vases, Egyptian mummies and paintings of Flemish village celebrations by Pieter Bruegel the Younger all add up to one of Europe's finest small museums. The Fitzwilliam grew out of a bequest by the 7th Viscount Fitzwilliam of Merrion in 1816 – £100,000 along with books and paintings. Today, free lectures and concerts are regular attractions, and the museum café is a favourite Cambridge meeting place.

WICKEN FEN Where can you find more than 200 bird species, 1,400 kinds of beetle, 1,000 categories of moth and 1,700 types of fly? Wicken Fen is the place – the National Trust's first nature reserve, set up in 1899 when it looked as if drainage for agriculture would abolish East Anglia's primal wetland.

As you approach, the 245ha (605 acre) fen appears as a dark-coloured island of undisciplined tree foliage in a neat sea of chemical-green grain prairie. Strolling its grassy walkways, you soon see that the island is an oasis. Willows and birches are full of bunting song; lagoons and streams ring with coot and waterhen cries. Ponds wrinkle with ripples from water spiders and beetles. There are rare birds such as marsh harrier and water rail, and wigeon in winter by the skyful. To witness the hum and buzz of insect and bird activity at Wicken Fen is to experience something long vanished from the surrounding landscape.

FITZWILLIAM MUSEUM ➡ Trumpington Street, Cambridge.
WICKEN FEN ➡ Signposted in Wicken village on A1123.

EAST ANGLIA
Essex

BULMER BRICKWORKS You would not be surprised to see hobbits at work around the cylindrical kiln at Bulmer Brickworks, with its mossy cone-shaped roof puffing out smoke among the trees like a house in an enchanted forest. The brickworks is a curious survival from an era before mass-production. It produces small numbers of specialised items for particular jobs, especially bricks and tiles of odd shape needed for the restoration and repair of historic buildings, such as Hampton Court Palace and Windsor Castle. The seams of clay from which the Bulmer bricks are made have been in almost constant use since Tudor times.

GREENSTED LOG CHURCH The squat nave of St Andrew's Church is made of great oak logs split in half, dark with age and weathering. They probably date back to very early Norman times, making St Andrew's the oldest wooden church in the world. It is said that in 1013 the body of St Edmund (martyred in AD 870 by the Danes) rested in an earlier church on the site on the journey to its final burial place at Bury St Edmunds. On the church wall hangs a 15th-century painting of the martyrdom, with the smiling saint stuck full of arrows while scowling Danish archers prepare to finish him off.

BULMER BRICKWORKS ➡ Signposted off minor road, 1 mile SW of Bulmer Tye, between Castle Hedingham and Sudbury.
GREENSTED LOG CHURCH ➡ 1 mile W of Chipping Ongar off A414.

KELVEDON HATCH SECRET NUCLEAR BUNKER

Step into this unassuming bungalow and you will soon be 24.4m (80ft) underground, deep inside a Cold War nuclear bunker, built in 1952. Behind blast-proof doors, 600 people could hope to live through a nuclear war, with supplies lasting for three months. It was anticipated that its occupants would be top military and civilian officials, including possibly the prime minister. Explore the warren of rooms that would ensure man's survival in a new world.

SOUTHEND PIER

Running out well over a mile into the Thames estuary, the pier is a breathtaking sight on its thousands of spindly centipede legs. The present iron pier replaced an earlier wooden one, first opened in 1830. It was completed in 1889 at the height of the Victorian seaside boom and stands today as a survivor of several disastrous fires and collisions with ships.

In spite of enormous changes in holiday habits, Southend Pier remains a magnet. Little red-and-white trains rattle the holidaymakers out to the pierhead where, beyond the café, the lifeboat station can be visited. The procession of giant ships near at hand, negotiating the Thames Estuary, tells you why the lifeboat is there.

KELVEDON HATCH SECRET NUCLEAR BUNKER ➡ Signposted off A128 from Chipping Ongar to Brentwood.
SOUTHEND PIER ➡ Southend seafront.

EAST ANGLIA
Norfolk

GRIME'S GRAVES Nine metres (30ft) below the surface, your feet meet solid ground and in the half-light you see a rough-hewn arch leading to a gloomy gallery. This is the bottom of one of more than 300 shafts sunk into the heathland of Thetford Forest. In the Dark Ages, people took this for a vast burial ground dug by Grim, a giant pagan god. Today's exhibition centre reveals Grime's Graves (EH) for what they really are: entrances to flint mines, excavated in the chalk around 3,500–4,000 years ago. Once underground, cold archaeological fact gives way to a feeling of kinship with the miners who worked the seams of grey nodules: source of axeheads, arrowheads, and other weapons and cutting tools in the days before iron.

NORFOLK LAVENDER For an exhilarating assault on your eyes and nose, go to Norfolk Lavender on a hot day in July before the hundred acres of flowers are harvested. With an immense carpet of purplish blue stretched out under a clear sky and the air laden with scent, you can imagine yourself in the plant's Mediterranean homeland. Lavender thrives at Heacham, which is one of the driest spots in Britain and has ideal soil conditions. You can see lavender oil being distilled, and buy deliciously smelly soaps and perfumes.

GRIME'S GRAVES ➡ 7 miles NW of Thetford off A134.
NORFOLK LAVENDER ➡ Caley Mill, Heacham, 2 miles S of Hunstanton on A149.

SAINSBURY CENTRE FOR VISUAL ARTS Set beside the River Yare, this gallery-cum-museum was revolutionary when built in 1978 and still impresses today. Norman Foster created it for the art collection of Sir Robert and Lady Sainsbury, designing it so that the metallic ribs of its skeleton are part of the visual effect. The eclectic collection lives up to the promise of its showcase exterior. Exhibits by sculptors from Henry Moore to African tribal artists stand beside Egyptian artefacts, carvings from South American civilisations and paintings by Picasso and Modigliani.

SCOLT HEAD ISLAND The short boat ride from Burnham Overy Staithe to Scolt Head Island (NT) transports you to a different world. Leaving creeks and mudflats behind, the boat – which operates from April to September – eventually arrives at a bleak hook of dune, shingle and salt marsh 3½ miles long. The silence is overwhelming, until thousands of gulls, waders and terns break into raucous protest.

The island has sand dunes higher than houses and is home to one of Britain's largest tern colonies. All three species of this pretty seabird, with a distinctive forked tail, breed here: the common tern, with scarlet legs and matching, black-tipped beak; the black-crested sandwich tern, with a yellow-tipped black dagger of a beak; and the rarer little tern, which has a bill and legs of all-over yellow.

SAINSBURY CENTRE FOR VISUAL ARTS ➡ At University of East Anglia, 2 miles W of Norwich, signposted off B1108 in Earlham.
SCOLT HEAD ISLAND ➡ A149 Hunstanton to Wells-next-the-Sea road.

Suffolk

BURY ST EDMUNDS, THE NUTSHELL It is claimed that more than 100 drinkers once squeezed into this tiny pub. The story takes some believing as the 16th-century building measures less than 5m by 2m (16ft by 7ft) – and there is certainly no room for more than half a dozen customers at the bar. But it is a friendly watering hole, even if you do find yourself nose to nose with a mummified cat or have to work out how to drink your pint with someone else's elbow in it.

HOUSE IN THE CLOUDS You see strange things in the resort of Thorpeness – not least what looks like a weatherboarded cottage, under a steeply pitched roof, perched 26m (85ft) above the ground on top of a five-storey house. The house is genuine enough, but the cottage is a disguised water tank, fed by a pump housed in a windmill alongside. It was built to supply water to the resort.

Stuart Ogilvie, a local landowner who was as much eccentric as inventive, began work on Thorpeness in 1910 by digging The Meare, an ornamental lake. The village, rich in mock-Tudor half-timbered houses, took shape over the next 20 years and today it functions exactly as Ogilvie intended – as a quiet coastal hideaway.

BURY ST EDMUNDS, THE NUTSHELL ➧ The Traverse, Abbeygate Street.
HOUSE IN THE CLOUDS ➧ 2 miles N of Aldeburgh, at end B1353.

LAVENHAM
Park the car and walk – Lavenham is so steeped in history that anything mechanical seems out of key. Its crooked streets are lined with the finest collection of timber-framed houses in England. Their painted beams, wonky plaster walls and lattice windows recall a time when everything was handmade from local materials.

For 150 years, from the 14th to the 16th centuries, this was a boom-town, the prosperous centre of Suffolk's wool trade. As trade grew, artisans acquired cottages of wood and plaster, while wealthy cloth merchants built on a grander scale. When Lavenham lost its hold on the trade in the 16th century, the town slowly crumbled until restoration began in the 19th century. Some 300 buildings are now listed.

ORFORD NESS
Europe has other vegetation-supporting shingle spits, but none is bigger than Orford Ness (NT). It is a moody and mysterious place thronged with nesting seabirds, reachable only by ferry and visited by few. Stand in the dips of the spit, with shingle rising on all sides, and you can feel truly cut off. Succeeding storms have thrown up lines of pebbles to form the shingle, which lies in row upon row of furrows, with colourful flora, including pink sea thrift and the rare sea pea.

From 1913 until the 1980s, the Ness was used for secret weapons testing. The strange, lonely atmosphere of the spit is somehow enhanced by its scatter of gaunt observation towers,

LAVENHAM ▶ 5 miles NE of Sudbury on A1141.
ORFORD NESS ▶ By ferry from Orford Quay, on B1084 E of Woodbridge (off A12).

barracks and 'pagoda' buildings where atomic bomb casings were tested. The gaps between the slender pillars were filled with perspex, which in the event of an accidental explosion would have been blown out, forcing the blast upwards into the dense concrete roof.

SUTTON HOO When a grassy mound in a Suffolk field was dug up in 1939, it revealed a 7th-century burial ship 28m (92ft) long. This was the grave of King Raedwald of East Anglia and inside was Britain's finest hoard of Anglo-Saxon treasure, including fabulous jewels and weapons. The site of Sutton Hoo (NT) offers a dramatic re-creation of the burial and displays of original objects loaned from the British Museum in London.

TATTINGSTONE WONDER From the back, it is a pair of ordinary red brick cottages. Walk round to the front and – hey presto! – it looks just like a medieval parish church, complete with a sham tower. Edward White of Tattingstone Place gave the Tattingstone Wonder its ecclesiastical frontage in 1790 so that he and his guests would have something dignified to look at from windows of his mansion.

SUTTON HOO ➡ On B1083 2 miles E of Woodbridge.
TATTINGSTONE WONDER ➡ On S shore of Alton Water reservoir, S of Tattingstone village, off A137 between Ipswich and Brantham.

CENTRAL

ENGLAND

CENTRAL ENGLAND
Derbyshire

ARBOR LOW Arbor Low (EH) is the Stonehenge of the North: an isolated, embanked Neolithic stone circle, over 4,000 years old. In this remote spot, nothing intrudes between the imagination of the visitor and an almost tangible sense of mystery clinging to the stones – 46 huge toppled slabs.

The magnificence of the location adds to the sense of awe. Lying at a height of 375m (1,230ft), Arbor Low has all-round views across the surrounding Peak District National Park – a country of far horizons, beneath wide skies echoing to trilling skylarks and the lonely call of curlews. A couple of fields away, and constructed at around the same time, lies the burial mound or barrow of Gib Hill.

CHATSWORTH PARK The grounds of the dukes of Devonshire's home contain many memorable man-made features, starting with the Emperor Fountain. Built in 1844 by Joseph Paxton, this is the world's highest gravity-fed fountain, shooting water 80m (260ft) into the air. Paxton also developed elaborate glasshouses at Chatsworth, including one for exotics that incorporates a Conservative Wall – so called because it has a system of flues and hot-water pipes which conserve heat for the plants. After Paxton's powerful water feature, the Willow

ARBOR LOW ▶ 5 miles SW of Bakewell off Youlgreave-Parsley Hay minor road.
CHATSWORTH PARK ▶ 8 miles N of Matlock off A6 Bakewell road.

Tree Fountain is a gentle affair, raining a shower of water from its copper branches. The stainless-steel, lily-shaped 'Revelation', created in 1999 and added to the Jack Pond, has water-powered petals that open and close around a golden sphere. More naturalistic is the stretch of the River Derwent that flows past the house – diverted to this course in the 1760s by the landscape-gardener 'Capability' Brown.

CROMFORD, CROMFORD MILL A grey fortress-like building on the Derwent is one of industrial history's most important sites. It was here in 1771 that Richard Arkwright, attracted by the potential of the river for supplying power, established the world's first successful water-powered cotton-spinning mill.

A large labour force working with powered machinery in a factory environment set the pattern for industrial development all over the world and earned Arkwright the title of 'Father of the factory system'. Alongside the factory an entire village was built. Only Cromford's remoteness and poor communications stopped it becoming another Manchester.

Cromford is one of the The Derwent Valley Mills, which were granted World Heritage Site status in 2001.

CROMFORD, CROMFORD MILL ➡ 10 miles N of Buxton off A6 Stockport road at New Mills.

MILLENNIUM WALKWAY On one side you can touch the sheer stone embankments and rock faces of the gorge, on the other just a handrail separates you from a fall to the swirling River Goyt, 6m (20ft) below. A walk along the elegant stainless-steel structure's 160m (175yd) length, opened in 2000, presents a thrilling experience, where the river's roar blocks out every other sound and its dappled reflections play among the overhanging trees of The Torrs Riverside Park. A heritage centre in New Mills, the town above the gorge, has descriptions of the valley's watermills and spinning industry.

PEAK CAVERN The most extensive network of Derbyshire caves lies at the head of the Hope Valley, where the limestone of the White Peak meets the shales and gritstone of the Dark Peak. People lived for 400 years in the gaping maw of Peak Cavern, the largest cave entrance in Britain. Its community of rope-makers has long gone, although rope-making has been revived at the cave, along with its local name, The Devil's Arse. The river that issues from under the 76m (250ft) wide entrance crag was known as the River Styx, and when the cavern flooded, as it does every winter, locals said it was the Devil relieving himself. Inside, you stoop to reach Roger Rain's House, named for its cascade of water, and the Orchestra Chamber, where concerts are held. Beyond, where no visitors venture, is Britain's deepest cave, the 152m (500ft) deep Titan.

MILLENNIUM WALKWAY ➡ 10 miles N of Buxton off A6
Stockport road at New Mills.
PEAK CAVERN ➡ Castleton, off A6187.

Gloucestershire

CHEDWORTH ROMAN VILLA For a Roman army officer planning to build a smart new villa in about AD 120 the wooded combe at Chedworth, overlooking the lovely valley of the River Coln, would have been the perfect site. It was just off the Fosseway and not too far from Glevum (Gloucester) or Corinium (Cirencester). Most important, it had a good supply of spring water – essential for the baths.

Over the next 300 years the villa evolved into an elegant mansion, complete with underfloor central heating, bathhouses and large reception rooms. Many of the fine mosaic floors survive, the best an example in the dining room depicting the seasons. Remains of the hypocausts, two bathhouses, including circular sweating chambers, and latrines with flushing water indicate the Romans' penchant for health and cleanliness.

Discovered by a local gamekeeper and first excavated in 1864, Chedworth (NT) provides fascinating evidence of how a Roman family set up home in England.

INTERNATIONAL CENTRE FOR BIRDS OF PREY

The most striking feature of the largest, most powerful owl in Europe is its orange eyes. This is no sweet little bird as it can kill a hare if necessary. It represents just one of the 25 species of

CHEDWORTH ROMAN VILLA ▶▶ 7 miles N of Cirencester off A429.
INTERNATIONAL CENTRE FOR BIRDS OF PREY ▶▶ S of Newent on B4216.

owl that are to be found at the International Centre for Birds of Prey, one of the most significant collections of birds of prey in the world. One of the centre's aims is conservation through a captive breeding programme, but the Centre also rescues and rehabilitates many birds.

Daily flying demonstrations allow visitors to appreciate the exquisite beauty and power of these birds, and winter owl evenings provide an opportunity to see the birds fly in the dark at a time which is natural to them.

KEMPLEY, ST MARY'S The interior of St Mary's (EH) is full of joyous colour.

In the early 12th century, when the church was built, hardly an inch of stone or timber was left unpainted. The chancel, beyond the finely carved Norman arch, is covered in frescoes glowing with pinks and terracotta. Christ sits on a rainbow on the vaulted ceiling surrounded by angels, the Virgin Mary, apostles and bishops, while in the nave the ten ages of man is represented in a circular Wheel of Life. They were painted in about 1120, probably for Hugh de Lacy, who fought at the Battle of Hastings, and are the most complete set of wall paintings of their kind in England.

Yet the church sits alone and officially redundant – a small, stubby-towered grey stone building with only ancient yew trees for company. Centuries ago the villagers of Kempley left for higher ground.

KEMPLEY, ST MARY'S ▶ 5 miles S of Ledbury off A449.

SEVERN BORE
There is a stillness, then a low roar. A huge wave, up to 2m (7ft) high, crashes upstream at about 10mph, clouting the banks with spray. Surfers ride its crest. It is as if the muscular brown River Severn has suddenly decided to flow the other way. Then it is gone, leaving the swollen river flowing upstream towards Gloucester. The Severn has the second highest tidal range anywhere in the world, and the configuration of the river bed causes the extraordinary phenomenon of the Severn Bore. Although it occurs on 260 days of the year it reaches its maximum height on only about 25, always near an equinox in spring or autumn.

The best places to see the Bore are at Minsterworth, Stonebench or Over Bridge. Severn Bore predictions are published annually and are given a star rating according to size.

WESTBURY COURT GARDEN
Not a leaf or twig is out of place at Westbury Court (NT); everything is in perfect order. Globes of holly and pyramids of yew are reflected in a long clear canal. A quincunx pattern (as in the five on a dice) of clipped evergreens and trees surrounds a Dutch pavilion with views across the River Severn. In 1696, when the garden was created, such formal Dutch designs were the height of fashion – their high cost, and the later vogue for 'Capability' Brown's natural landscaping, meant that few survived. This is the earliest example left in England, and none in Holland are as perfect.

SEVERN BORE ▶ Minsterworth, 4 miles W of Gloucester off A40/A48. Stonebench, 3 miles SW of Gloucester off A430/B4008. Over bridge, 1 mile W of Gloucester on A40.
WESTBURY COURT GARDEN ▶ 10 miles SW of Gloucester on A48.

CENTRAL ENGLAND
Herefordshire

CENTRAL ENGLAND Herefordshire

CROFT CASTLE AND CROFT AMBREY Fine avenues
of oaks, beeches and 350-year-old Spanish chestnuts lead
to Croft Castle (NT), set four-square on a high sweep of
border country with all the confidence of a fortress home first
mentioned in the Domesday Book. In the 18th century, the
house was given one of the earliest 'Gothick' makeovers.

On the 305m (1,000ft) high ridge behind Croft is the
Ambrey, where Celts farmed for 400 years before the Roman
conquest. You can see 14 counties from their camp. Here, in
AD 50, the chieftain Caratacus faced the legions of Rome.

EASTNOR CASTLE If you were to dream of a castle,
this is probably how it would look. Eastnor is huge and
symmetrical, with clover-leaf towers at each corner and
a battlemented tower in the middle. Castellated terraces
descend to a broad lake and red deer graze in 122ha
(300 acres) of parkland below the Malvern Hills. Yet the
castle was built in the early 19th century, not in the 12th.
It is essentially a pastiche, a copy of a medieval fortress, built
by Robert Smirke, architect of the British Museum, for the
1st Earl Somers between 1810 and 1824. Somers wanted to
impress his contemporaries. Succeeding generations added

CROFT CASTLE AND CROFT AMBREY ➤➤ 5 miles NW of
Leominster off B4362.
EASTNOR CASTLE ➤➤ 2 miles E of Ledbury on A438.

94

to the interiors – the Gothic drawing room was designed by A.W.N. Pugin and J.G. Crace, collaborators on the Houses of Parliament – and today Eastnor is an elegant family home.

KILPECK CHURCH Real and imaginary beasts like the Basilisk, hatched from a cock's egg by a toad, and the
Mantichore, a lion's body with a man's head, leap from the exterior arches of Kilpeck church. The 12th-century church has survived from a time when few people could read, but everyone understood images. Sculptors drew on Celtic, Saxon and Viking imagery to create sexually explicit figures, such as the Sheela-na-Gig (a woman exposing her genitalia, thought to be a fertility symbol) as well as huntsmen and dragons. Inside the church there was peace, personified by carvings of serene saints.

MAPPA MUNDI Dimly lit in a cabinet of Derbyshire slate in Hereford Cathedral, the *Mappa Mundi* – a 13th-century
world map – offers a glimpse of medieval learning. Drawn on vellum (calfskin) in about 1290, it presents the world in spiritual and geographical terms, with Jerusalem at the centre. Dragons are illustrated here, as are cities and towns, and images of people, plants, angels and devils, headed by Christ sitting in judgement. In one corner is a horseman on what was a white horse, until a medieval boy decorated it with neat spots.

KILPECK CHURCH ➡ 9 miles SW of Hereford, signposted from A465 between Hereford and Pontrilas.
MAPPA MUNDI ➡ In New Library, Hereford Cathedral.

CENTRAL ENGLAND

Leicestershire & Rutland

CLIPSHAM YEW TREE AVENUE A regiment of exotically clipped yew trees lines the drive to Clipsham Hall. Many of the 150 ancient trees are crowned with sculpted topknots or animals, including an elephant and a deer. Some designs represent historic events, such as a Battle of Britain Spitfire or Neil Armstrong's Moon landing in 1969. The trees are trimmed into shape each September, using powered hedgecutters and mechanical hoists – advantages denied to Amos Alexander, the head forester of Clipsham estate, who started this unusual project in 1870.

NATIONAL SPACE CENTRE A transparent Rocket Tower of super-light plastic material hooped with curved steel tubes erupts 42m (138ft) above the car park like an alien chrysalis – the sleek form of the Blue Streak rocket visible inside. Next to it, the Space Theatre's futuristic geodesic dome occupies an old storm water tank. Six themed galleries give you the chance to experience aspects of space travel – here you can launch a rocket, build a satellite or join the crew of a lunar base. The collection of space gear and technology may make you ponder the big questions. Where do we come from? Is anybody else out there?

CLIPSHAM YEW TREE AVENUE ➡ 1 mile E of A1, 8 miles N of Stamford, just outside Clipsham, near Ram Jam Inn.
NATIONAL SPACE CENTRE ➡ 1 mile N of Leicester city centre.

RUTLAND WATER When Rutland Water was created in the 1970s, it was western Europe's largest man-made lake, covering 1,255ha (3,100 acres), or 4 per cent of Rutland, England's smallest county. Besides huge quantities of water for the expanding East Midlands, it provides a spacious outdoor leisure playground and a haven for wildlife, including osprey.

On the lake's southeastern shores, Normanton church is preserved as a poignant reminder of the impact the rising waters had on the surrounding community. Just the tower and clerestory remain visible above the waterline. Inside, a small museum traces the history and geology of the reservoir. Walks and cycle tracks follow the lake's 25 mile perimeter, but its scope and scale is best appreciated from a boat.

RUTLAND WATER ▶ 2 miles E of Oakham.

Rutland Water

TAYLOR'S BELLFOUNDRY AND MUSEUM From

a ladle nearly as big as a man, molten metal heated in a furnace to 1,200°C is poured into a mould set in a sandpit to cast a new bell. When Great Paul, the 16 tonner that hangs in St Paul's Cathedral, was cast at Taylor's in 1888 it took two weeks to cool.

Taylor's is a family firm founded in 1838 when the bells of All Saints Church in Loughborough needed recasting. It is the world's largest working bellfoundry. Church bells, hand bells, ships' bells and carillons are made or restored here. A tour reveals the intricate process of bell-making, from preparing the core of the bell mould using sand, hay and horse manure, to the art of inscribing, the thrill of casting and the skill of tuning.

TAYLOR'S BELLFOUNDRY AND MUSEUM ▶▶ Freehold Street, Loughborough.

BOSTON STUMP The good folk of Boston wanted the world – or at least every sailor for miles out to sea, and every landlubber on the fens – to know their town was the greatest port after London, so they built the highest church tower in England. It was started in the early 1300s and eventually, some 200 years later, a halt was called. By then, the tower had reached a giddying 83m (272ft). In a masterpiece of understatement some wag gave it the sobriquet, the Stump. Inside, the nave pillars tilt on silty foundations, and the misericords on the choirstalls depict medieval domestic scenes, such as a teacher birching a pupil who has a book stuffed in his breeches.

GRIMSTHORPE CASTLE It could be said that Grimsthorpe Castle is all front – but what a front. Part of a larger design by the architect John Vanbrugh, the great north front (1726) is a superb Baroque version of a medieval fortress, symbolic of the 16th Baron Willoughby's ambition to reflect his new status as a duke in the ancestral home. Soaring above the roof line, colossal statues on classical themes crown great Tuscan pillars and frame a huge family coat of arms. Beyond the main entrance, the heroic theme continues in a spectacular arcaded hall before you enter the human huddle of the house.

BOSTON STUMP ➡➡ Boston town centre.
GRIMSTHORPE CASTLE ➡➡ 5 miles NW of Bourne on A151.

NATIONAL FISHING HERITAGE CENTRE A tour of the trawler *Ross Tiger* with a former trawlerman evokes the treacherous conditions on its fishing expeditions: the exhausting shifts, freezing decks, whiplash cables and the deafening roar of the engine room.

It is one of the highlights of a visit to the National Fishing Heritage Centre in Grimsby, the world's largest fishing port in the 1950s. The Centre captures the essence of this hazardous trade in recordings, tableaux and story boards with bracing icy blasts, moving decks and salty aromas.

For more fishy experiences join a tour to Grimsby's early morning fish auction, with a visit to a traditional dockside smoke-house.

STAMFORD The A1 takes a swing around it, but you should turn off and visit this lovely town – in 1967 it was the first in England to declare itself a conservation area. Stamford has more than 500 listed buildings of architectural or historic merit. No wonder it is a favourite backdrop for period costume dramas.

Many houses have the beautifully proportioned, trademark windows of the Georgian era. But some of Stamford's buildings, such as the almshouses, Browne's Hospital (1483), in Broad Street, belong to the years when the town was a prosperous cloth port on the River Welland. In a maze of

NATIONAL FISHING HERITAGE CENTRE ▮▸ Alexandra Dock, Grimsby.
STAMFORD ▮▸ 1 mile E of A1 on Lincs/Cambs border.

medieval streets, the roofs are a particular delight: some have graded tiles that become smaller and thinner as they climb to the ridge; others are clad in frost-fractured Collyweston limestone, subtly shading from blue to brown.

THE WASH Thousands of seals, wading birds and wildfowl inhabit the remote, marshy flatlands and shingle beaches of The Wash. Rare plants, amphibians and insects colonise the shore – marsh orchids, natterjack toads and 12 species of dragonfly among them. Their movement, calls and song may be the only signs of life in these vast expanses of land. Nature reserves at Gedney Drove End, Frampton Marsh, Freiston Shore and Gibraltar Point provide access points, trails and information about the fragile ecosystem.

The North Sea took a broad, square bite from the low-lying coastline between Skegness and the bulge of East Anglia to form The Wash. Rivers draining into this shallow basin added peat and alluvium to tidal scourings deposited by the sea, and the region slowly silted up – Boston, once England's second largest seaport, now lies four miles inland. Vast areas of saline marshland have been reclaimed since the Romans built sea banks and drains along the silt ridges near Holbeach. Today, a system of banks, dykes and pumps protects the area. But visitors should take care not to leave the sea banks as tidal flows are swift and dangerous.

THE WASH ▶▶ From Skegness to Hunstanton.

Northamptonshire

GEDDINGTON, ELEANOR CROSS A tall stone monument encrusted with carvings

stands in Geddington village. Three statues decorate its niches, each representing Eleanor of Castile, wife of Edward I. This is the best-preserved of three surviving crosses erected in 1294 by the grief-stricken king to mark the places where Eleanor's funeral cortège rested overnight on its way south to London. Eleanor and Edward wed in 1254, and during their 36-year marriage the couple were rarely apart. In 1290, when Edward set off to fight the Scots, Eleanor followed but, already gravely ill, she died at Harby, Nottinghamshire.

HARRINGWORTH VIADUCT A startling landmark strides across the wide floodplain of the Welland

between Harringworth and Seaton. The Harringworth railway viaduct's 82 arches rise 18m (59ft) above the valley floor, extend for ¾ mile and contain some 15 million bricks. Two thousand men worked on the viaduct between 1876 and 1878 to carry the Midland Railway's branch line between Kettering and Manton. The full impact of this colossal structure is best experienced from a distance. Occasional trains are diverted across the viaduct and special-steam train excursions are organised, but it no longer carries regular passenger services.

GEDDINGTON, ELEANOR CROSS ➡ 3 miles N of Kettering on A43.
HARRINGWORTH VIADUCT ➡ 12 miles SW of Stamford off A47/B672.

Two thousand men worked on the viaduct
between 1876 and 1878

In The
Shape
of a Shoe

NORTHAMPTON MUSEUM Kitten heels, absurd creations of the 1970s and even an elephant boot used in an expedition of 1959 to re-create Hannibal's crossing of the Alps are among the 12,000 outlandish items of footwear held at Northampton Museum. The shoe-making town has possibly the world's largest collection of historic footwear – so big that only a selection can be shown at any one time. Dazzlingly impractical court shoes with 15cm (6in) heels play footsie with the desiccated remnants of Roman shoes unearthed in archaeological digs, Queen Victoria's silk wedding shoes, electrically heated flying boots and parachute boots with built-in shock absorbers.

ROCKINGHAM CASTLE Stout drum towers flanking the entrance confront visitors with the perfect image of a stalwart medieval fortress. Step through the gate, and you progress three centuries to find gabled, honey-coloured buildings resembling a Tudor estate. Rockingham Castle has assumed many guises and combines with architectural flair a mix of styles chronicling the needs of its successive occupants – from the remains of the original fortified walls (now a terrace giving glorious views over five counties) to the 17th-century laundry adorned with clock and bell-tower. Inside, mementos of Charles Dickens commemorate his visits to the castle, the model for Chesney Wold – home of the Dedlocks in the novel *Bleak House*.

NORTHAMPTON MUSEUM ▶ Guildhall Road, Northampton.
ROCKINGHAM CASTLE ▶ 1 mile N of Corby off A6003.

CENTRAL ENGLAND
Nottinghamshire

HODSOCK SNOWDROPS In the dark days of February, long before the garden-visiting season begins in most places, Hodsock Priory is besieged by visitors. For a few fleeting weeks, winter woodland in the 324ha (800 acre) grounds lies under drifts of snowdrops, intermingled with the yellow of winter aconites, green-tinged hellebores or Christmas roses, and the mauves and hot yellows of early crocuses.

LAXTON Dry and dusty history lessons! Remember the teacher talking about the medieval open field system? What did it look like, this England without its patchwork of small fields and hedges? At Laxton, you can find out, for this is the only place in Britain where it is still possible to see and walk the rolling acres of a feudal past.

Three great open fields, first recorded in around 1200, surround the village. Here, on 810ha (2,000 acres), the serfs, villeins and freemen of Laxintune, as the Domesday Book called it, ploughed long, thin strips of land in ways still copied by Laxton farmers today. In another reminder of the village past, an ancient manorial court meets to check the field boundaries and adjudicate in disputes. There is a visitor centre at the Dovecote Inn with further information.

HODSOCK SNOWDROPS ➡ 1 mile SW of Blyth (on A1), off B6045 (Blyth-Worksop road).
LAXTON ➡ 3 miles SW of Tuxford on A1.

NOTTINGHAM CAVES

Underneath the city of Nottingham lies a honeycomb of caves — more than 400 in the centre alone. All were scraped by hand from the soft sandstone mound on which the city stands. An escalator leading into a basement shopping precinct provides an improbable access point.

Visitors are directed through 14 different caverns, variously used throughout the centuries as storage areas and dwelling places, prisons, air-raid shelters and secret meeting rooms. One cave was used as a tannery. Another section re-creates the appalling slum conditions endured by Nottingham's Victorian poor. Other caves are accessible from Nottingham Castle.

SOUTHWELL, THE WORKHOUSE

Tiny top-floor windows, rows of lavatories, distempered walls and circular scars on the kitchen floors where huge coppers boiled cabbage, potatoes and tea — many stark details reveal the bleak history of Southwell's former workhouse (NT). Built in 1824, it housed the poor for 150 years, and was the prototype for more than 600 workhouses built after the 1834 Poor Law Amendment Act.

Its plain façade and regimented interior embodied the severe philosophy that shaped treatment of the poor. Inmates were segregated into classes, families were split up and men, women and children kept apart. Life was controlled and monotonous. It was the very system that drove Charles Dickens to write *Oliver Twist*.

NOTTINGHAM CAVES ➠ Under Broad Marsh Shopping Centre. Ye Olde Trip to Jerusalem, 1 Brewhouse Yard, Nottingham.
SOUTHWELL, THE WORKHOUSE ➠ On outskirts of Southwell, off A612.

UPTON HALL TIME MUSEUM Step inside this elegant Georgian mansion

and you enter a world of unsynchronised ticking, clanking and chiming, as dozens of timepieces mark the passing hours. Upton Hall is home to the British Horological Institute. The largest collection of clocks and watches in Britain is displayed in its reception rooms. Prize exhibits include 'Tim', the original speaking clock, and the atomic 'BBC pips' machine. Sniff out a Chinese incense clock, but don't set your watch by the exhibits – many are more than 300 years old and their accuracy cannot be guaranteed.

WORKSOP, MR STRAW'S HOUSE You will feel a sense of disbelief

when you stand outside No. 7 Blyth Grove, Worksop. Is this unexceptional, early 20th-century semi really owned by the National Trust? Only once beyond the bay window and panelled front door does all become clear: No. 7 is a time capsule, exactly as it was when well-to-do grocer William Straw moved there in 1923, having first had the house refurbished in the style of the day.

After William and his wife died, their sons kept everything exactly as Dad and Mum had left it, down to the Sanderson wallpapers, grained woodwork and Axminster staircarpet with its fashionable Tutankhamun motifs. Nothing was thrown out – as larder shelves lined with tins of treacle and bottles of salad cream, and neatly tied bundles of the parents' letters testify.

UPTON HALL TIME MUSEUM ➡ 3 miles N of Southwell, on A612.
WORKSOP, MR STRAW'S HOUSE ➡ Worksop signposted from Blyth Road (B6045).

CENTRAL ENGLAND
Shropshire

HAWKSTONE PARK AND FOLLIES So striking and otherworldly is Hawkstone Park that it served as the backdrop

for a television adaptation of C.S. Lewis's *Chronicles of Narnia*. Set among rugged sandstone hills, the 40ha (100 acre) park with its caves, dizzying clifftops, glades and eerie rock formations offers a surprise at every turn. Adding to the visual feast is an array of follies, including the thatched Gingerbread Hall and the 34m (112ft) high Monument. Hawkstone Park is the creation of the Hill family, who owned it until 1906. They added fantastic constructions and walks to the park's natural features. In the late 18th century they published a guide to Hawkstone that encouraged visitors from across England and Wales, so staking a claim to be the creators of the world's first leisure theme park.

LUDLOW With a medieval street plan and nearly 500 listed buildings, Ludlow can rightfully claim, as a local guide book

says, to be 'one of Europe's most beautiful towns'. Nowhere is this more apparent than on Broad Street, where you can stroll through nearly 1,000 years of history. Beginning at the elegant Georgian town houses close to the River Teme, you pass timbered buildings from the 14th to 16th centuries, still in active use, as you climb to the robust castle, completed in 1086.

HAWKSTONE PARK AND FOLLIES ➡ Weston-under-Redcastle village, near Hodnet, off A53 or A49, 11 miles N of Shrewsbury.
LUDLOW ➡ 24 miles N of Hereford off A49.

Edward IV's sons, later the 'Princes in the Tower', were raised here, and it was the venue for the premiere of John Milton's masque *Comus* in 1634.

STOKESAY CASTLE A Jacobean timber-framed custard-coloured gatehouse marks the entrance to Stokesay Castle (EH), a fortified manor house built in the Onny Valley by a wealthy wool merchant 700 years ago. Lawrence of Ludlow was keen on home comforts by 13th-century standards. He built a 16m (52ft) long Great Hall with a central fireplace. After meals the family would retire upstairs to a wood-panelled solar, or drawing room, with peep holes onto the hall below. Decorative tiles, mullioned windows and delicate carvings abound, such as a Flemish 17th-century overmantel.

THE LONG MYND More than 30 miles of footpaths criss-cross The Long Mynd (NT), an area of undulating heathland offering spectacular views to the Brecon Beacons and sightings of moorland birds such as stonechat. The ridge-top track, the Portway, has been in use for thousands of years, and Bronze Age burial mounds dot the hillsides. Lovers' Walk, so called because of the many kissing gates placed along its length, culminates at a natural spring – the 'pop works'. The bubbling waters were once believed to treat sluggish livers, gout and obesity.

STOKESAY CASTLE ➡ 7 miles NW of Ludlow off A49.
THE LONG MYND ➡ The Long Mynd rises W of Church Stretton off A49, 12 miles S of Shrewsbury.

THE WREKIN The Wrekin looms like a stranded sea monster above the Shropshire Plain, rising abruptly to 407m (1,335ft). From the top, reached by a relatively easy climb, there are matchless views across the surrounding country – on a clear day you can see 17 English and Welsh counties. Legend has it that many of its most prominent features are the work of two giants who still live beneath its surface.

The Wrekin's name is derived from the Celtic terms *wre* and *ken*, meaning 'most conspicuous hill'. The ancient British Cornovii tribe recognised the hill's strategic value, making it their capital.

WROXETER ROMAN CITY One of the largest examples of Roman masonry still standing in Britain can be seen at Wroxeter (EH). Known as The Old Work, the 8m (26ft) high wall formed part of a basilica, or gymnasium, in Viroconium, the fourth-largest Roman settlement in the province.

The city had developed from a simple fortress established around AD 58 beside the Roman road of Watling Street to become an impressive urban area of 5,000 inhabitants in the 2nd century. Laid out in a grid pattern on the banks of the River Severn, the site contains extensive remains, including the underfloor heating system of a bathhouse, and parts of a market hall and tavern. Many of the artefacts found on the site can be seen in the museum.

THE WREKIN ➠ S of A5, 10 miles E of Shrewsbury.
WROXETER ROMAN CITY ➠ 5 miles E of Shrewsbury off A5.

On a clear day you can see 17 English
and Welsh counties

CENTRAL ENGLAND
Staffordshire

CHEADLE, ST GILES Even the ornate spire and red west doors with their magnificent gold lions – family emblem of the Earl of Shrewsbury, patron of St Giles – do not prepare the visitor for what lies within. What was lost when churches were stripped of their decoration in the Reformation? What sights greeted the 13th-century peasant on the Sabbath? At St Giles, in what has been called the outstanding English church of the 19th century, the architect A.W.N. Pugin, still only 29 years old, gave genius and imagination full rein to re-create the age of Decorated Gothic. Every inch of the interior is sumptuously decorated with gleaming metalwork, gorgeously painted walls and glowing floor tiles.

FIELDS OF REMEMBRANCE The statue of a blindfolded soldier stands in the National Memorial Arboretum at Alrewas. Private Herbert Burden lied about his age to join up and was only 17 when he was shot for desertion in the First World War. Nearby are memorials to the 1941-5 campaign in the Far East. A replica length of track and a plinth commemorate those who died on the Sumatra Railway. An original section of line, with sleepers and spikes, honours the 16,000 Allied servicemen who died during construction of the infamous Burma Railway.

CHEADLE, ST GILES ➡ Cheadle town centre, 10 miles E of Stoke-on-Trent off A52 Ashbourne road.
FIELDS OF REMEMBRANCE ➡ National Memorial Arboretum, Alrewas, 4 miles NE of Lichfield signposted off A38 or A513. Commonwealth and German cemeteries, 2 miles N of Cannock off A34 Stafford road.

Twelve miles away, near Broadhurst Green on Cannock Chase, there are more reminders of those who fell in the last century's conflicts. The lawns of the Commonwealth War Cemetery contain 97 white headstones for First World War servicemen, mostly New Zealanders. In the larger German Military Cemetery, ranks of granite headstones mark the 5,000 combatants of that nation who died on British soil. They include the bodies of airship crews from the 1914-18 conflict, those of aircrews shot down in the Second World War and dead German seamen washed up on British beaches.

THOR'S CAVE Film-makers needing a location for prehistoric man have often looked no farther than Thor's Cave. It is the archetypal caveman's dwelling, a gaping void high on a limestone crag above the River Manifold. Early Victorian archaeologists were the first to discover that this many-chambered, many-fissured cavern, named after the Norse god of war, provided just such a home for our Stone-Age ancestors. As you stand at the entrance and admire the Manifold Valley below, you can imagine how they must have scanned the same magnificent landscape, perhaps in search of game.

Thor's Cave can be reached by a stairway from the Manifold Valley. This path follows the course of one of the Peak District's disappearing rivers, which sink into deep cracks in the limestone.

THOR'S CAVE ➡ Near Wetton, off A523, 10 miles SE of Leek.

CENTRAL ENGLAND
Warwickshire & West Midlands

BARBER INSTITUTE OF FINE ARTS Dame Martha Constance Hattie Barber did not live to see the realisation of the dream that she and her property-developer husband shared of a grand public building housing a world-class art collection and concert hall. She died in 1932, a few months after bequeathing the family fortune to the institute and seven years before the austerely elegant, stone-and-brick Art Deco building in the grounds of Birmingham University opened.

The galleries contain a fabulous collection of paintings, from Renaissance masterpieces by Bellini and Botticelli, to Impressionist works by Monet and van Gogh, and 20th-century pieces by Picasso and Magritte. There are sculptures and miniatures, and a collection of coins, seals and weights.

PACKWOOD HOUSE Graham Baron Ash, the wealthy son of a Birmingham industrialist, restored 16th-century Packwood House (NT) in the 1930s: it contains his collection of furniture, tapestries and paintings. But it was an earlier owner who created the property's most impressive feature. In the 1670s, John Fetherston, whose grandfather built Packwood,

BARBER INSTITUTE OF FINE ARTS ➡ 3 miles SW of Birmingham city centre off A38 Bristol road.
PACKWOOD HOUSE ➡ 9 miles NW of Warwick off B4439 Hatton-Hockley Heath road.

planted the Yew Garden. There are more than 100 trees, representing the Sermon on the Mount. The smallest trees were planted in the 19th century and symbolise the crowd. These lead to a lawn where The Apostles, a group of 12 yews, grow. Beyond them, on a hump, is The Master (Christ) – a solitary tree approached along a spiral path lined with box hedging. It takes three gardeners three months to clip the entire topiary.

STRATFORD-UPON-AVON Surprisingly little is known about William Shakespeare,

but at Stratford you can get as close as is possible to the great writer and gain an insight into English life at the turn of the 17th century. The interiors of Shakespeare's birthplace, a house he inherited in 1601, are alive with the bright colours and patterns of their restored furnishings. The playwright would also have known the finely carved timber frontage of Harvard House in the High Street. Built in 1596 by Thomas Rogers, grandfather of the founder of Harvard, America's oldest university, it now houses an incomparable collection of pewter. Just beyond it is Nash's House in Chapel Street, next to the site of New Place where Shakespeare spent his last years. Nash's House is furnished as New Place might have been. At Wilmcote, outside Stratford, is a hamlet of two houses where Shakespeare's mother, Mary, lived. They compose a charming evocation of rural life and history.

STRATFORD-UPON-AVON ▪▸ All in centre of Stratford – except Mary Arden's House, 3 miles N of Stratford, signposted off A3400.

WARWICK CASTLE Few castles rival the scale and grandeur of Warwick. The original motte and bailey fort was built here by William the Conqueror in 1068, just two years after the Norman Conquest. Today, the castle towers over the River Avon, dominating the unspoilt town at its feet, just as the 1st Earl of Warwick – the so-called Kingmaker – dominated the kings of the 15th century. Its vast gardens and grounds were one of 'Capability' Brown's first commissions, for the Greville family who owned the castle from 1604 to 1978. Inside, you witness history in a series of brilliantly conceived tableaux, from a 14th-century dungeon to a Victorian weekend party.

This is not just the story of kings and noblemen. The Kingmaker exhibition re-creates the preparations for a Wars of the Roses battle in 1471, when the 1st Earl died fighting Edward IV's army at Barnet. Here, wheelwrights, longbowmen and seamstresses all come to life. You may also witness the firing of the castle's trebuchet, a huge catapult.

WARWICK CASTLE ➡➡ **Warwick town centre, off A46, 2 miles from M40 (Junction 15).**

CENTRAL ENGLAND
Worcestershire

DROITWICH BRINE BATHS Can't swim? Don't worry.
With 1.1kg (2½lb) of salt in every warm gallon of water –
ten times the concentration in seawater – the brine baths are
just the solution to buoy you up. They owe their existence
to an underground lake 60m (200ft) below the town, a sort
of subterranean Dead Sea. In the 1830s, the original baths
made the town a fashionable health resort, and their modern
replacements, opened in 1985, are still a popular way to rise
above life's cares.

HARVINGTON HALL The finest series of priests' hiding
places anywhere in Britain have been revealed at Harvington
Hall. In the reign of Elizabeth I at the end of the 16th century,
when to be a Roman Catholic priest was to commit high
treason, the clerics found refuge at this safe haven. They were
secreted under the oak stairs, above a bread oven, and in the
rafters and walls. Some of the priest holes are known to be the
work of Nicholas ('Little John') Owen, master builder of such
hiding places. In 1606 he was starved out of one of his own
hides and tortured to death in the Tower of London.

The moated, russet-brick house, set among lawns with
stables and a church, is an evocative fragment of Elizabethan

DROITWICH BRINE BATHS ➠ S of Droitwich town centre, off A38
Worcester road.
HARVINGTON HALL ➠ 3 miles SE of Kidderminster, ½ mile E of A450.

England. Inside is a puzzle to be unravelled – an atmospheric warren of rooms, staircases and passageways intricately decorated with late 16th-century monochrome wall paintings.

ROYAL WORCESTER PORCELAIN WORKS The transformation of a lump of wet clay into an item of fine china is fascinating. At the Royal Worcester Porcelain Works you can see all the stages – a process essentially unchanged since production started in 1751 – down to the painting by hand of exquisitely detailed fruit-and-flower decorations.

Adjoining the oldest porcelain factory in England is a museum containing examples of Royal Worcester ware. There are grand coronation plates, high quality tableware, ornamental vases and porcelain figures, all beautifully crafted.

WITLEY COURT Kings and courtiers were entertained at Witley Court (EH) in conditions of the most extravagant luxury. Today, this magnificent Palladian palace is but a ruin, destroyed by fire in 1937. Yet the first sight of what lies beyond its roofless skeleton never fails to bring a gasp of delight.

The Earl of Dudley lavished attention on the property in its heyday in the 19th century. The gardens, designed by William Nesfield around a stone fountain set in a shining lake, have been restored to their former splendour.

ROYAL WORCESTER PORCELAIN WORKS ➽ Severn Street, S of Worcester city centre.
WITLEY COURT ➽ 10 miles NW of Worcester on A443.

NORTHWEST

ENGLAND

Cheshire & the Wirral

ANDERTON BOAT LIFT A bewildering array of pillars, pulleys and pistons is an ingenious solution to a complex problem: how to lift canal boats 15m (49ft) from the River Weaver into the Trent and Mersey Canal. Two enormous boat-carrying tanks, or caissons, are used in the operation. Each caisson weighs 252 tonnes when full of water and 80 tonnes when empty.

At rest, one tank is level with the canal and the other is level with the river. To move the tanks, a small amount of water is removed from the bottom tank. As the heavier top tank descends, it forces hydraulic fluid into a connected cylinder on the lighter tank, pushing it upwards. Built in 1875, the Anderton Boat Lift was the world's first boat lift and is still the only one of its kind in England.

DEE ESTUARY Climb the footpath up the hill which rises behind the half-timbered, thatched cottages of Burton village and you will be rewarded with panoramic views across the vast stretches of mudflats, sand and salt marsh of the Dee Estuary. The village of Burton once served as a port for boats to and from Ireland, but as the Dee silted up it lost its position on the coast, and the area became instead a port of call for a

ANDERTON BOAT LIFT ➡ In Anderton off A533. Signposted for 2½ miles from centre of Northwich.
DEE ESTUARY ➡ Burton Mill Wood, 3 miles SE of Neston off A540.

different type of visitor. The estuary provides a winter refuge for more than 100,000 wading birds: two-thirds of Britain's over-wintering wildfowl. As the tide goes out, it reveals a feeding ground for a vast array of species. October heralds the peak period for shelduck, redshank and curlew, and in December ragged flocks of lapwing make spectacular patterns against the winter sky.

JODRELL BANK A 76m (249ft) dish, weighing 3,200 tonnes, towers above the Cheshire Plain.

This is the Lovell Telescope at Jodrell Bank – the world's second-largest fully steerable telescope. Radio waves emitted by objects in space are collected by the dish and converted into signals that are used to map distant stars and galaxies. The telescope is capable of recording Cosmic Microwave Background Radiation, the oldest type detected by any radio telescope, originating 300,000 years (a mere split second in evolutionary terms) after the Big Bang.

Completed in 1957, the Lovell Telescope has discovered quasars (intense, star-like sources of radio waves) and researched pulsars (the collapsed cores of supergiant stars). Its visitor centre will take you on a tour of outer space.

JODRELL BANK ➡ Signposted from the M6, Junction 18.

LITTLE MORETON HALL **Lopsided windows, imperfect right-angles and a carp-crowded moat all contribute** to the architectural charm of Little Moreton Hall (NT). It is one of the finest examples of a timber-framed, moated building in England, and it seems miraculous that its three storeys, with their bulging walls, are still standing. The earliest sections of the house, including the porch, Parlour and Great Hall, were built in 1450–80. In the 1560s, the Long Gallery was added, causing the walls of the south wing to bend and bow outwards under its weight. Look above the doorways for exquisite wood carvings and above a window the inscription of Richard Dale, a carpenter who worked here in the 1550s.

PORT SUNLIGHT **The neat cottages and gardens, spacious streets and open areas of this model village** have a rural serenity: a place of peace and quiet, built by William Hesketh Lever, later Lord Leverhulme, for workers at his adjoining Sunlight soap factory. The village reflects his interests in architecture and town planning. The original layout was his, and he paid close attention to the designs of the 30 architects who worked on the 900 houses – most of which were completed during the 1890s and early years of the 20th century. On The Diamond, in the village centre, Lord Leverhulme built the Lady Lever Art Gallery in memory of his wife. Its works of art include Pre-Raphaelite paintings and Chinese porcelain.

LITTLE MORETON HALL ➧ **4 miles SW of Congleton on A34.**
PORT SUNLIGHT ➧ **2½ miles SE of Birkenhead off A41 Chester road.**

NORTHWEST ENGLAND
Cumbria

APPLEBY HORSE FAIR Caravans and cars line the byways for miles around as gypsies from all over Britain converge on Fair Hill in Appleby on the second Wednesday in June. They come for the final day of the annual Horse Fair, first held in 1685. Horse-trading is the essential business of the week-long event, but other activities from farriery (shoeing horses) to harness racing have grown up around it.

Visitors flock to the little town to see horses being washed in the River Eden, buy lucky charms, have their fortunes told and wander among some of the 200 stalls. But the fair has not turned into a commercial show – everyone gets caught up in the romance of the occasion.

BLACKWELL The house's stark, rather austere clifftop presence above Lake Windermere gives little clue to the wealth of finely crafted detail and glowing jewel-like colour to be found inside. The architect M.H. Baillie created Blackwell in 1897-1900 as a country home for the Manchester brewer, Sir Edward Holt. All of its original Arts and Crafts features have survived remarkably intact. After the First World War, the Holt family rarely used the house. Later, it served as a school, then as offices. During this time, the décor was boarded over

APPLEBY HORSE FAIR ➡ On B6542, S of A66 between Penrith and Brough.
BLACKWELL ➡ 1½ miles S of Bowness-on-Windermere, on B5360, off A5074.

NORTHWEST ENGLAND Cumbria

130

or hidden behind filing cabinets. Then the Lakeland Arts Trust bought and restored Blackwell. In 2001 all was revealed and the restored rooms are again free to dazzle and delight.

BURGH-BY-SANDS, ST MICHAEL'S The walls of Burgh church's 14th-century tower are 1.5m (5ft) thick,

with slits for windows and no outside door. Such fortification is evidence of violent border disputes between the Scots and English. The only entrance to the tower is within the church through a yett (a heavy iron gate). Inside, you find yourself in a gloomy cavity, where locals once huddled in fear, overlooked by shadowy stone carvings of mysterious beasts. Unnerving carvings that lurk above the lintel have been interpreted as a hippopotamus and an elephant, but whoever shaped the stones could not have seen such animals. Perhaps the carver dreamt of them – they certainly possess an otherworldly quality.

St Michael's stands squarely within the bounds of a Roman fort and is built entirely of its stone. Edward I's body was brought here for temporary safe-keeping in 1307 after he died leading his troops to do battle with the Scots in one last weary campaign across the Solway Firth. In the years that followed, villagers built the strong bell-tower to protect themselves from the Scottish enemy.

BURGH-BY-SANDS, ST MICHAEL'S ➡ 6 miles NW of Carlisle, N of Moorhouse off B5307.

CASTLERIGG STONE CIRCLE

CASTLERIGG STONE CIRCLE On days of dank mist, the standing stones of Castlerigg Circle (NT/EH) seem to brood, while on crisp mornings of scudding cloud they shiver and dance. Level ground is a rarity in the Lake District, so the people who chose this spot for their ritual site made the most of it. That was at least 5,000 years ago. The circle comprises 38 roughly hewn standing stones. All around are high fells and mountains. The effect is to turn the sky into a hemisphere, with you and the stones at its centre. The time of day, time of year, winds and weather all change the look and feel of the place. What it all meant in the Bronze Age remains a mystery, but it is hard now not to make up your own magic.

CASTLERIGG STONE CIRCLE ➼ 2 miles E of Keswick, via layby on minor road to Naddle Bridge.

Castlerigg Stone Circle

HIGH CUP NICK Nothing prepares you for the moment you find yourself at the 'nick' (head) of **High Cup Gill** on the brow of the Pennine moors. It is one of the pivotal points on the spine of England, overlooking the finest views and set in the wildest landscape. A chasm opens out below you and great curved faces of rock sweep away to create an amphitheatre-like bowl. A stream disappears into the verdant Eden Valley, and beyond lies the grandeur of the Lakeland fells. High Cup is on the route of the Pennine Way – well signed from Teesdale. For a really enjoyable walk, take a friend, choose a clear day and arrange for someone to collect you so that you can cover the whole section one way, a distance of just over 13 miles.

HIGH CUP NICK ▣▸ Forest-in-Teesdale, on B6277 between Middleton, Alston and Dufton, off A66 N of Appleby.

The circle comprises 38 roughly hewn standing stones

Isle of Man

BALLAUGH CURRAGHS **Following the boggy trails that wind through the strange, wet wilderness** of the Ballaugh Curraghs is like walking through a fairytale landscape. Lichens drip from the branches of twisted and gnarled willows, which dip their fronds in the secret, still pools of the 81ha (200 acres) of waterlogged former peat cuttings. Overhead, a wraith-like shape hovers over the reed beds – it is a hen harrier, an elegant marshland raptor. Up to a hundred pairs of hen harriers roost here in winter – the largest number in Western Europe. The Curraghs are also home to peregrine falcons, merlins, grasshopper warblers and greylag geese.

LAXEY WHEEL **The world's largest working water wheel continues to function** long after the mine it served closed down. Engineer Robert Casement was employed by Captain Richard Rowe to construct the 22m (72ft) diameter wheel to pump water from Rowe's profitable Great Laxey lead mine in the hills above. Casement then applied his architectural skills to embellish and transform the wheel into a popular and much-admired monument of Victorian engineering.

The great, white-painted circular tower, complete with a 95-step spiral staircase leading to a dizzily exposed viewing

BALLAUGH CURRAGHS ➡ Off A3 Ramsey–Kirk Michael road near Ballaugh.
LAXEY WHEEL ➡ Laxey can be reached by Manx Electric Railway from Douglas or Ramsey, or by minor road off A2 Ramsey–Douglas road.

platform over the top of the wheel, serves no practical purpose. But ever since its opening in 1854, it has attracted thousands of visitors. To this day, many arrive on the narrow-gauge Manx Electric Railway that runs along the coast between Douglas and Ramsay. Getting off at Laxey, they walk past a row of miners' cottages, known as Ham and Egg Terrace because of the refreshments its residents used to provide for visitors. The wheel is named Lady Isabella, after the wife of the island's governor, the Hon. Charles Hope, who set it in motion at its inauguration.

TT RACES The roar of motorbikes careering around the Isle of Man's normally quiet roads at speeds of more than 120mph is a thrilling annual experience. The island's population expands by more than half each June as 40,000 biking enthusiasts arrive to witness the famous TT (Tourist Trophy) races. They take place on a twisting, tortuous 38-mile route that encircles the island and winds high over a shoulder of Snaefell mountain using public roads. When the Auto Cycle Club organised the first TT races for motorbikes in 1907, the winners averaged less than 40mph. The story of the TT races is described in the Manx Museum in Douglas.

TT RACES ▶ TT course marked by orange signs.

Lancashire, Liverpool & Manchester

ALBERT DOCK Completed in 1845, the Albert Dock was one of the most impressive pieces of commercial building of its time, big enough to accommodate the biggest merchantmen of the day. In the 1980s, the disused dock was given a new lease of life. There are restaurants and shops in the quayside colonnades of its five-storey former warehouses – Britain's largest group of Grade I listed buildings. The Tate Liverpool art gallery and Merseyside Maritime Museum are located here, as is The Beatles Story – an exhibition about the 'fab four'.

BLACKPOOL With ten white-knuckle rides, including the original 1923 Big Dipper, Blackpool is Britain's roller-coaster capital. At 72m (236ft) high, the Pepsi Max Big One is the country's tallest roller-coaster and reaches speeds of 87mph. For a ride through water, fire, blizzards, flaming arrows, spooky forests and an icy graveyard, take the Valhalla. The railway brought the first trippers to Blackpool in 1846. More than 16 million people flock to Britain's gaudiest seaside resort each year to enjoy the Pleasure Beach, the piers, the Tower (built in 1894 to imitate the Eiffel) and the illuminations from September to November.

ALBERT DOCK ➡ ¼ mile SW of Liverpool city centre.
BLACKPOOL ➡ M6 (Junction 32), then M55.

CHETHAM'S LIBRARY Humphrey Chetham, a wealthy Manchester businessman, founded the library named after him in 1653 to 'cure poverty by curing ignorance'. Since then, it has been in constant use. For the social, political and economic theorist Karl Marx, it was a place to study and to meet and share ideas with Friedrich Engels, founder of 'scientific socialism'. The simple desk that they used can still be seen. Today, the library holds more than 100,000 volumes, of which some 60,000 are more than 150 years old.

MERSEY FERRY After more than 800 years, the Mersey Ferry – propelled to fame by the 1960s pop song 'Ferry 'Cross the Mersey' – continues to ply the broad river and offer the best way to see the sights of Liverpool. For thousands of emigrants bound for America in the late 19th century, this was their last view of England. The port of Liverpool was then second only to London in size and importance.

Among the prominent features of today's skyline are the Anglican Cathedral – Britain's biggest, started in 1904 to a design by Giles Gilbert Scott and completed in 1978. Majestic waterfront edifices include the Royal Liver Building of 1911, topped by the city's symbol: two 5.5m (18ft) tall copper Liver Birds, half cormorant, half eagle. The Liver Building's clocks, each 8m (26ft) in diameter, are the largest in Britain and said to be correct to within 30 seconds a year.

CHETHAM'S LIBRARY ▶ Long Millgate, Manchester.
MERSEY FERRY ▶ Liverpool city centre.

MORECAMBE BAY

Hugely empty and lonely save for thousands of wading birds, Morecambe Bay is a vast expanse of up to 120 square miles of glistening sand laced with pools. Only the foolhardy would risk the tide and attempt alone the ancient right of way across the Kent Channel from Morecambe to Kents Bank in Cumbria. Instead, Cedric Robinson, the official Queen's Guide and so-called Sand Pilot of Morecambe Bay, leads walkers safely to Kents Bank from Hest Bank or, more usually, Arnside.

RUFFORD OLD HALL

It has long been held that William Shakespeare performed in this area of Lancashire as a young actor and appeared at Rufford Old Hall (NT) for the owner, Sir Thomas Hesketh, in the 1580s. Be that fact or fiction, the stage in the Great Hall remains as a tangible reminder of the heyday of this house.

Rufford is one of the best remaining examples of a late medieval timber-framed hall. The elaborate black-and-white Tudor building is largely unchanged since it was built in the 15th century and contains fine collections of arms and armoury, tapestries and 17th-century furniture. The mood of the whole is preserved in the surrounding garden, adorned with sculpture and topiary.

MORECAMBE BAY ➡ W of M6 (Junction 34/35A) or A6. Hest Bank, 2 miles N of Morecambe on A5105. Arnside, 10 miles N of Morecambe on B5282, off A6.
RUFFORD OLD HALL ➡ 5 miles N of Ormskirk on A59.

NORTHEAST

ENGLAND

BOWES MUSEUM Coming across a flamboyant French chateau in deepest Durham is enough to make you gasp in disbelief. The scope of the art inside will make you think you have been transported to a major gallery in a great metropolis. John Bowes was passionate about all things French, including his wife, Josephine. Hence the style of the building that he erected on his Durham estate to house his vast collection of fine art and crafts. Sadly, the chateau, completed in 1892, took 23 years to build, by which time both John and Josephine were dead.

The Bowes' obsession with collecting is reflected in the diversity of works. French decorative art dominates, with a musical automaton of a life-sized silver swan taking centre stage. But there are also tapestries and paintings by Tiepolo and El Greco, dolls' houses and even Bronze Age swords.

DURHAM CATHEDRAL The Normans built their greatest cathedral as a resting place for St Cuthbert, the North's best-loved saint. They believed in big buildings, but at Durham they combined their monumental, solid style of architecture with an Anglo-Saxon love of decoration and detail. The result is an inspiration. Built between 1093 and 1133, the cathedral is substantially unaltered. The extraordinary Galilee Chapel, built

BOWES MUSEUM ➡ Off A688 in Barnard Castle, 16 miles W of Darlington.
DURHAM CATHEDRAL ➡ Palace Green, Durham city centre.

in the style of a Moorish mosque, contains the tomb of the historian and monk, the Venerable Bede. Double bays and thick, fluted, highly patterned columns support the nave. Walk beyond the crossing and rib-vaulted transepts to the choir, the tomb of St Cuthbert and the Chapel of Nine Altars. An undercroft just off the cloister contains St Cuthbert's Treasures – among the golden chalices and seals is the saint's original 7th-century coffin, a jigsaw of oak fragments with a tracery of incised figures of apostles, angels and the Virgin and Child. The contrast between the fragile remains of the saint's coffin and the power and permanence of its setting is profound.

HARTLEPOOL HISTORIC QUAY The masts of a grand sailing frigate, dating back to 1817, tower over the quay.

The oldest British warship afloat, HMS *Trincomalee* was brought to Hartlepool in 1987 and restored by local craftsmen. Around it, chandlers, gunsmiths, a jail and an admiral's house re-create the heyday of a Napoleonic seaport. Dramatic re-enactments, including a ghost's tour of a sea battle and virtual reality exhibits, bring the scene vividly to life. Watch a press gang in action, or play traditional games in Skittle Square. For a taste of the seafaring life, climb on board *Trincomalee*. The adjacent museum and adventure centre allow you to walk the lower decks of a blood-and-thunder warship in battle, or to test your reflexes at rat-catching duties.

HARTLEPOOL HISTORIC QUAY ➤➤ Hartlepool town centre, off A689, 8 miles NE of Stockton-on-Tees.

HIGH FORCE Whisky-coloured water from peat-capped fells in the northern Pennines is tossed and buffeted down the River Tees in a succession of pretty cascades. Then, suddenly, rushing over bare, craggy cliffs, it plunges 22m (72ft) – the longest single water drop in England. This fierce and noisy waterfall is High Force.

There are two ways to view the falls. The quickest, and the easiest, is to pay a small fee at the car park next to the High Force Hotel, then take the 10-minute signposted walk down the track to the foot of the falls. From here, steps lead steeply to the top, where you can pause for breath, enjoy the cooling caress of spray, and gaze on the foamy, swirling water as it thunders into the shadowy plunge pool in the gorge below. For an even more picturesque route, through grassy fields and woodland, you can park at Bowlees Picnic Area and stroll upstream beside the Tees. This walk should take about 1½ hours there and back.

MIDDLESBROUGH, TRANSPORTER BRIDGE
The biggest transporter bridge in the world operates across the River Tees between Middlesbrough and Port Clarence. It was devised in 1911 as an ingenious alternative to a drawbridge, to allow the passage of tall-masted ships. A gondola, which can carry nine cars and up to 100 people, is suspended below a high cantilever structure and winched

HIGH FORCE ▶ 5 miles NW of Middleton-in-Teesdale off B6277.
MIDDLESBROUGH, TRANSPORTER BRIDGE ▶ Between Stockton-on-Tees and Middlesbrough off A66 and A1046.

across the water every 15 minutes. The bridge is 259m (850ft) long, and the height from low-water level to the girders is about 54m (177ft).

SALTBURN INCLINED TRAMWAY Every few minutes a gurgle and a rush of water is followed by a gentle lurch. Then the two red 10-seater tram cars glide silently past each other on their brief journey up and down the cliff face at Saltburn-by-the-Sea. Some things around Saltburn have changed over the past century, but the cliff lift looks as stylish today as it did when it opened in 1884 – and it is still going strong.

Until the mid 19th century, Saltburn had been a fishing and smuggling village, but the entrepreneur Henry Pease saw an opportunity to develop it into an upmarket seaside town. The Stockton–Darlington Railway was extended from Redcar in 1861, and Saltburn soon had its own promenade and pier, croquet lawn, Italian gardens and spa fountain.

Huffing and puffing up and down a cliff path between the pier and the seafront hotels was beneath the dignity of Victorian gentry. The solution for the newly invented holiday resort was the building of a hydraulic tramway, 36m (118ft) long, powered by a gas pump and 91,000 litres (20,000 gallons) of water.

SALTBURN INCLINED TRAMWAY ➡ Opposite Saltburn pier, 4 miles S of Redcar on A174.

NORTHEAST ENGLAND

Northumberland & Tyneside

ANGEL OF THE NORTH

ANGEL OF THE NORTH Antony Gormley's colossal angel, completed in 1998, is already etched into the psyche of northeast England. It stands immutable, 20m (66ft) tall and with a 54m (177ft) wingspan, on a ridge close to the A1 and the East Coast railway line at Gateshead. More than 30 million people are thought to see it every year. On its grassy knoll, the angel looks poised for take-off. Walk up to the ridged iron feet and you are standing over cleared mine workings, atop a plinth capping the steel piles that bond the statue to the bedrock.

GATESHEAD QUAYS

GATESHEAD QUAYS Once a bustling heartland of industry, the newly revitalised Gateshead Quays have become an impressive arts and cultural space. A 1950s grain warehouse is home to the BALTIC Centre for Contemporary Art, a provocative world where visual art is created as well as viewed. In contrast architecturally is Sage Gateshead, a building of steel and glass with a spectacular curved roof. This enormous venue, designed by Foster and Partners, is the new home for live music in the North of England, with performance spaces, rehearsal rooms, teaching areas, studios and an educational centre.

ANGEL OF THE NORTH ➨ Leave A1 at Gateshead South/ Birtley exit onto A167 and park in layby.
GATESHEAD QUAYS ➨ Newcastle Gateshead Quays.

HOLY ISLAND The thick walls, tall columns and flowing arches of the 12th-century Lindisfarne Priory on Holy Island (EH) mark the spot where, in 635, St Aidan founded a Christian settlement that grew in size and status to become a focal point for Anglo-Saxon art and learning. The monastery also became a target for Viking raids and was destroyed in 793. A 9th or 10th-century gravestone in the little visitor centre depicts Doomsday as a gang of Vikings.

Holy Island is so steeped in historical significance that it is easy to miss its unspoilt shoreline and rich wildlife. It is best taken at an easy stroll, around the harbour to Castle Point and back to the village and the ruins of the monastic buildings. The causeway to the island is impassable at high tide.

KIELDER SKYSPACE Colours and tones drift almost imperceptibly.

At dawn or dusk the quality of light in the landscape changes second by second. American artist James Turrell's 'Skyspace' is intended to make us look at something we do not usually pay much attention to: light.

The installation is a half-buried cylindrical chamber on a hilltop in Kielder Forest. You sit on concrete seats to appreciate the visual effects from a 3m (10ft) wide hole in the roof. After a few minutes, the smooth walls of the chamber become part of the experience. There is a balance between interior and exterior light and the perfect disc of sky seems to turn to ice, pearl or steel, washed by subtle shades and unusual colours. Out onto the hilltop again and the sky may look completely different. The spell is broken as you stumble back down the track in the twilight.

ST MARY'S LIGHTHOUSE AND ISLAND Climbing the 137 steps to the top of St Mary's Lighthouse

will make you puff, but on a sunny morning the coastal view is dazzling. The little island lies just offshore from Curry's Point – which commemorates a murderer gibbeted here in 1739 – and was remote enough to attract medieval hermits. The lighthouse, opened in 1898, has always been a popular seaside stroll from Whitley Bay. The traditional thrill of waiting until the last minute to beat the tide back over the causeway remains undiminished.

HOLY ISLAND ▶▶ 7 miles S of Berwick-upon-Tweed off A1.
KIELDER SKYSPACE ▶▶ Access by track from car park signposted to left, off Kielder Water, 15 miles W of Bellingham off B6320 and 2 miles SE of Kielder.
ST MARY'S LIGHTHOUSE AND ISLAND ▶▶ 1 mile N of Whitley Bay off A193.

BEMPTON CLIFFS The setting is dramatic – an RSPB visitor centre and viewpoints perched at the summit of 122m (400ft) cliffs, with lighthouse-topped Flamborough Head nearby. The sound is deafening – thousands of noisy seabirds flying to and from their nests. It adds up to one of the most memorable wildlife experiences in Britain.

Thirty-three species of seabird breed at the Bempton Cliffs reserve, including fulmars, gannets, guillemots, kittiwakes, puffins and razorbills. April to July, when they are raising their chicks, is the best time to come. Puffins are the most endearing of the cliffs' residents, but gannets put on the best display: gleaming white darts of swept-back wing and spear-like beak as they plunge-dive to catch fish. The gannets have their only mainland colony at Bempton.

FIVE RISE LOCKS An impressive staircase of locks on the Leeds and Liverpool Canal is one of the wonders of the entire British canal system. With a steep rise of 18m (59ft) in five stages, it is a complex and – to inexperienced boat-handlers – daunting obstacle to negotiate. Each lock is 20m (66ft) long and 4.4m (14ft 5in) wide, with the top gate acting as the bottom gate of the next, so it is impossible

BEMPTON CLIFFS ➡ 5 miles N of Bridlington off B1229.
FIVE RISE LOCKS ➡ 5 miles E of Keighley. Signposted from centre of Bingley off A650.

to empty a lock unless the one below is empty. The whole system holds 409,000 litres (90,000 gallons) of water.

The 127-mile Leeds and Liverpool Canal was first proposed by a group of Bradford businessmen keen to transport their wares to the seaport of Liverpool. It was built between 1770 and 1816. Until 2001, and the reopening of the Huddersfield Narrow Canal, it was the only waterway to cross the Pennines. Walk along the towpath to the west for wonderful views of the mills and surrounding hills, including Rombalds and Ilkley Moors.

HOW STEAN GORGE Raised walkways and footbridges on three different levels take you above the rushing waters

of How Stean Beck, and through a world of 24m (79ft) high overhanging cliffs, dark caves and dripping vegetation. The narrow, twisting gorge feels so otherworldly that it has been chosen as the setting for science-fiction dramas, including *Doctor Who* and *Blake's Seven*. If you feel daring, descend the narrow wooden steps into Tom Taylor's Cave, and scramble out into Cat Hole Field at the other end. The gorge was formed by the erosive effects of melting Ice Age glaciers. Unequal erosion between harder and softer limestone created the caves and the odd rock formations inside them.

HOW STEAN GORGE ➡➡ 7 miles NW of Pateley Bridge on minor road to Lofthouse.

HUMBER BRIDGE The statistics alone are amazing: **44,120 miles of wire for the cables and 480,000 tonnes** of concrete for the two towers and roadway. At 1,410m (4,626ft), this was the longest single-span suspension bridge in the world when it opened in 1981. But the masterpiece of civil engineering is far more than a list of big numbers. The latticework of cables and the tall ladder-like towers add up to a strikingly graceful as well as monumental structure. And there are impressive small numbers, too: the towers are 36mm (1½in) farther apart at their tops than their bases – compensation for the curvature of the Earth.

SALTAIRE As you wander around Saltaire you might believe you are in Bologna, not Bradford. This complete Italianate model township was the creation of Sir Titus Salt, a local wool-stapler. Salt earned a vast fortune by importing alpaca wool from South America to create a cloth that was more lustrous than other woollens. It became hugely popular, especially when Queen Victoria began to wear it. Salt combined his name with that of the local River Aire to create a title for the town that he built between 1853 and 1876 for his factories and his workers and their families.

The first building to be constructed was a magnificent, mansion-like mill that could produce 27,000m (30,000yd) of cloth a day. It now houses shops and galleries, including

HUMBER BRIDGE ➠ 6 miles W of Kingston upon Hull.
SALTAIRE ➠ 4 miles NW of Bradford off A650.

the 1853 Gallery, which has Europe's largest collection of work by the Bradford-born artist David Hockney. Near it is the sumptuous Congregational Church, completed in 1859, which has a fine entrance portico with six Corinthian columns and an octagonal tower. Nearly 800 workers' houses, a hospital and public baths were built at Saltaire. Look out for images of llamas (or alpacas) – part of Salt's coat of arms – which adorn many buildings.

YORK MINSTER Northern Europe's biggest Gothic cathedral impresses not only with its sheer magnificence and size, but in its detail. Its glories range from superb medieval stained-glass windows – the largest collection in Britain – to the bright modern bosses in the roof of the south transept, reconstructed after a disastrous fire in 1984. Overall, the Minster is a remarkable example of 13th and 14th-century architecture lovingly preserved.

For a breathtaking panorama over the city to the rolling countryside beyond, climb the 275 steps to the top of the central tower. Back at ground level, a walk around the 13th-century city walls also reveals York's Roman and Viking past, while the overhanging eaves of streets such as The Shambles give a taste of medieval times.

YORK MINSTER ▶▶ High Petergate, York city centre.

WALES

North & Mid Wales

BARMOUTH BRIDGE Forget the 500 timber piles that support the rail bridge across the mile-wide river mouth: look at the fabulous view. The Afon Mawddach possesses one of the loveliest estuaries of all the rivers in Wales. Along both shores, golden sand sweeps up to marshy pockets and woodland-stuffed valleys. Bare slopes emerge beyond, and higher up again lie the rugged mountains of Snowdonia – the Rhinogs to the north, Cadair Idris to the south.

Trains on the Cambrian Coaster railway stop on both sides of the bridge – at Morfa Mawddach Station and in Barmouth. Alternatively, payment of a small toll gives access to the footpath beside the track – part of the Mawddach Trail, which follows the route of a dismantled rail line inland along the southern shore of the estuary.

BEAUMARIS CASTLE Its squat walls, mirrored in the moat, give the fortress an almost welcoming demeanour. But appearances are deceptive, for this is the most technically perfect medieval castle in Britain. Begun in 1295, it was the last link in the ring of strongholds built by Edward I to crush the Welsh. Although funds ran out before it could be completed, the concentric system of defences (more than

BARMOUTH BRIDGE ▶▶ 1 mile NE of Fairbourne off A493 Dolgellau–Tywyn road (S side); E edge of Barmouth, off A496 Dolgellau–Harlech road (N side).
BEAUMARIS CASTLE ▶▶ Beaumaris, 4 miles NE of Menai Bridge on A545.

4 miles long) were state of the art. The inner boundary of the moat is lined by the low outer wall with 16 projecting towers, or bastions. Beyond this lies a narrow courtyard, overshadowed by the inner main walls, every inch of which is covered by massive projecting bastions and two formidable, towered gatehouses, which lie at opposite ends of the castle.

CAPEL SOAR In a country famous for its chapels, Capel Soar ranks as one of the most remarkable.

The solitary whitewashed building, which dates from 1822, lies deep in the Cambrian Mountains: a beacon for the devout sheep-farming communities of these remote uplands.

With the decline of the rural population in the past 50 years or so, the chapel's future looked grim, but its doors have remained open thanks to the efforts of local people. Regular services are held during the summer months. Its reputation as a place of simple devotion set in an elemental landscape has also spread. Where once a surrounding congregation would arrive on foot and by horse, visitors from as far afield as America, Argentina and Australia now draw up in cars. Inside, rows of plain wooden pews overlooked by a small pulpit match the exterior simplicity.

CAPEL SOAR ➡➡ Soar y Mynydd, 12 miles SE of Tregaron on minor road to Llandovery.

GREAT ORME MINES The Great Orme headland that
looms above the seaside resort of Llandudno has yielded up
an ancient secret: a maze of copper mines hewn by Bronze
Age man between 3,000 and 4,000 years ago. Since excavation
began in 1987, tonnes of spoil dumped by miners in the
18th and 19th centuries have been stripped away to reveal
a growing labyrinth of tunnels – the most extensive mine
discovered from the ancient world. The scale of the workings
is breathtaking, especially because the Bronze Age miners had
nothing but stone and bone tools with which to extract the
copper ore. The remains of these tools have been discovered
in large numbers, along with charcoal, which suggests they
weakened the mine face by first lighting fires against it.

PONTCYSYLLTE AQUEDUCT Those with a head for
heights can cross the Pontcysyllte Aqueduct, 39m (128ft)
above ground, by taking a trip on a narrowboat or walking
along the towpath. Thomas Telford built the imposing
structure in 1805 to carry the Llangollen Canal across the
valley of the Dee and link it with the rest of the Shropshire
Union. He used long cast-iron troughs to hold the water,
supporting them on masonry piers so slimly elegant that his
doubters thought the edifice would collapse. Nearly two
centuries later, it still transports boats for a dizzying 305m
(1,000ft) between one side of the valley and the other.

GREAT ORME MINES ➡ 1 mile NW of Llandudno off minor
road, or tramway to Orme summit.
PONTCYSYLLTE AQUEDUCT ➡ 4 miles E of Llangollen, off A5
Chirk road at Froncysyllte.

This surreal little world full of architectural jokes and influences

PORTMEIRION This has been described as the village where Wales becomes Italy, where the Mediterranean mixes with medieval Britain and the Orient. But words cannot quite capture the dazzling personality of this surreal little world full of architectural jokes and influences. The architect Sir Clough Williams-Ellis created the village between 1925 and 1972, taking a 'light-opera sort of approach' to the design. Pastel-coloured buildings of all shapes and sizes are scattered around a central piazza and ornamental gardens, and every turning reveals a fake façade.

SUMMIT OF SNOWDON The rocks at the top of the highest peak in Wales illustrate the almost inconceivable length of geological time. They contain the fossils of seashells, scattered over an ocean floor 500 million years ago, buried under volcanic ash, lifted by mountain-building forces and now exposed after aeons of erosion by water and ice. Ancient and worn down though it is, the 1,085m (3,560ft) summit (NT) is still a spectacular vantage point, with views south to Cadair Idris and west to Ireland.

Trains on the rack-and-pinion railway, which runs from Llanberis, make light work of the ascent, but there are several footpaths to the top. Best of these for seasoned walkers is the Watkin Path from the south – start from the Nantgwynant car park, 4 miles northeast of Beddgelert on the A498.

PORTMEIRION ▸ 3 miles E of Porthmadog off A487 Penrhyndeudraeth road.
SUMMIT OF SNOWDON ▸ 12 miles SE of Caernarfon off A4086.

WALES

South Wales

BARAFUNDLE BAY Barafundle (NT) is the perfect beach. It has rock pools, a clean sweep of sand reaching out to crystal-clear waters, high sand dunes, cliffs and rock stacks – and none of the things that spoil beaches: roads, car parks, arcades or electronic noise. Barafundle has no access for vehicles, no toilets or café. It is an isolated place, reached by a grassy footpath, unsullied and unrivalled.

BIG PIT NATIONAL COAL MUSEUM Former miner Colin switches out the lamps on the visitors' helmets. 'Just imagine how those ponies felt,' he says. Then he pauses before continuing: 'One week's holiday up at the surface every year; other than that, down here in the dark all their working lives.' At 90m (300ft) underground, Big Pit certainly is dark – the epitome of pitch-blackness. And it is draughty, too, thanks to air blowing down the ventilation shafts and whistling between the galleries. When the 120-year-old pit closed in 1980, the miners restored the workings – from which no coal had been extracted for a number of years – and opened the colliery as a visitor attraction, staffed and maintained by themselves and former mining colleagues. Big Pit stands on the edge of Blaenavon Industrial Landscape, now a World Heritage Site.

BARAFUNDLE BAY ▶▶ ½ mile walk from Stackpole Quay car park. Signposted from Stackpole off B4319.
BIG PIT NATIONAL COAL MUSEUM ▶▶ ¾ mile W of Blaenavon town centre.

CARDIFF MILLENNIUM STADIUM Imagine the roar of 72,500 Welsh people singing 'Bread of Heaven' at the tops of their voices as their 15 rugby heroes in red shirts run onto the pitch. That is the sound that shakes the awesome Millennium Stadium on match days when the Welsh team comes out to play. The stadium, which was opened just in time to host the 1999 Rugby World Cup, has a palletised pitch – just lift out any damaged section and drop in a new one – and a giant retractable roof. It cost £114 million to build and most Welsh people reckon it was worth the money.

CHEPSTOW CASTLE Like one cliff piled on top of another, the fortress rises from a bluff-bound spur in a bend of the River Wye. William FitzOsbern, brother-in-arms and powerful ally of William the Conqueror, began construction in 1067, within a year of the Battle of Hastings. His yellow-stone Great Tower is the oldest surviving Norman fortification in Britain, and some of its masonry dates back even further – the builders recycled stone from the old Roman town of Caerwent, 5 miles southwest of Chepstow. The centuries following the Norman conquest saw walls, towers, bastions and the magnificent 13th-century gatehouse marching along and around the castle's precarious perch above the river.

CARDIFF MILLENNIUM STADIUM ▶▶ Cardiff Arms Park, beside River Taff in city centre.
CHEPSTOW CASTLE ▶▶ Chepstow town centre.

ISLANDS Of the five accessible islands off the coast of Pembrokeshire, four are run as nature reserves and the fifth has a monastery. Lying farthest east, Caldey Island is the most tamed and civilised, but it possesses its full share of magic. Monks of the Reformed Cistercian (Trappist) Order own and run the island. They make and sell perfume, chocolate and other delights. Beyond the monastery are sandy beaches, farmland, woods and clifftop paths.

Skokholm Island (pronounced 'Skoe-k'm') was made famous in 1930 when naturalist and adventurer Ronald Lockley published *Dream Island*, a best-selling account of the life he and his wife Doris led as sole occupants. Small numbers of visitors are allowed onto the island to see the farmhouse that Lockley renovated with driftwood and explore the cliffs and paths. The island's turf is pierced by an estimated 86,000 burrows made by puffins, rabbits and Manx shearwaters. About 150,000 Manx shearwaters – half the world population – nest and breed on Skokholm and its sister island Skomer.

Ramsey Island is run as an RSPB reserve, with trails that allow you to explore its striking landscape. You might even spot the rare chough, with its brilliant scarlet beak and legs, which has re-established itself on the 120m (394ft) high cliffs.

Tiny Grassholm Island is a stronghold of the gannet. Eighty thousand of these big white fishing birds nest there. You cannot land on the island, but the stench, noise and sight from the cruise boat are overwhelming enough.

SKOKHOLM & SKOMER ISLANDS ➡ Crossings from Martin's Haven, signposted from B4327 via Marloes.
RAMSEY ISLAND ➡ Crossings from St Justinian, signposted from St David's on A487.

ST DAVID'S HEAD AND ARTHUR'S QUOIT

The rocky promontory of St David's Head is rich in prehistoric remains. Here, above 30m (100ft) cliffs, are the circular foundations of the huts of Iron Age farmers, the raised seams of their field boundaries and the line of a double wall known as the Warrior's Dyke with which they sealed off their dwellings from the world.

Less than a mile away is Arthur's Quoit. Locals say it was thrown here from a nearby hill by the legendary hero Arthur. Archaeologists believe that the enormous slab of stone is the capstone of a burial chamber some 5,500 years old. All that prevents it from slamming to earth is one slim, upright stone.

TINTERN ABBEY **Walking between the columns of the roofless abbey church,** you can easily see how it inspired the poet William Wordsworth and the painter J.M.W. Turner. Tintern's dove-grey ruins are intensely romantic: grass underfoot, the sky above, and beyond the great windows at either end of the nave, views of the Wye Valley. Little is left of the first Cistercian church, which was founded here in 1131; the remains that stand today date mostly from the last 30 years of the 13th century.

ST DAVID'S HEAD & ARTHUR'S QUOIT ➡ St David's Head, 3 miles NW of St David's. Path from end of B4583 at Whitesands Bay. Arthur's Quoit, ⅓ mile NE of St David's Head.
TINTERN ABBEY ➡ 5 miles N of Chepstow on A466 Monmouth road.

SCOTLAND

Central & Northeast Scotland

AONACH MOR **Even when the glens below Aonach Mor are bathed in spring sunshine,** a 15-minute ride by cable car takes winter-sports enthusiasts, climbers and sightseers to an alpine wonderland of ice and snow. There is a cafeteria at journey's end with colossal views across the Highlands, and chair lifts and walk routes lead still higher. From Aonach Mor's 1,221m (4,006ft) summit, you look out across a deep, intimidating corrie to the notoriously dangerous north face of Ben Nevis – Britain's highest mountain at 1,343m (4,406ft) above sea level.

BUTE, MOUNT STUART **The Isle of Bute in the Firth of Clyde is the setting** for one of Britain's most extraordinary monuments to high Victorian extravagance. Built between 1880 and 1900, Mount Stuart was the home of the 3rd Marquess of Bute, a lover of medieval architecture and said to be the richest man in Britain. His enthusiasm and fortune were devoted to the restoration of historic buildings, but his home was his own private fantasy: a place intended to astound, which it continues to do.

AONACH MOR ▶▶ 4 miles NE of Fort William signposted off A82.
BUTE, MOUNT STUART ▶▶ 5 miles S of Rothesay on A844 Kingarth road.

FINGAL'S CAVE

This great sea cave on the isle of Staffa has been compared to a grand work of architecture. After visiting in 1772, the naturalist Sir Joseph Banks described it as being far superior to any building of the ancient or modern worlds. Fingal's Cave does indeed resemble a man-made structure – a cathedral, with a 'nave' 70m (230ft) long by 13m (43ft) wide and walls some 18m (59ft) in height formed from hexagonal basalt columns. In place of organ music there is the surge and echo of the sea, a sound that inspired Felix Mendelssohn – who visited Staffa in the summer of 1829 – to compose his *Hebrides* overture.

FINGAL'S CAVE ➡ 8 miles N of SW tip of island of Mull. Frequent boat-trips all summer from Fionnphort, on Mull.

Fingal's Cave

HOLLOW MOUNTAIN A tunnel more than half-a-mile long takes minibus passengers from the shore of Loch Awe to a hydroelectric power station buried beneath Ben Cruachan. The cavernous Machine Hall – the height of a seven-storey building and the size of a football pitch – looks like a sci-fi film set. The plant is ingeniously designed to meet fluctuations in demand for electricity. If 10 million kettles are switched on during a commercial break, the generators whirr instantly to life, driven by water from the reservoir above. In off-peak periods, they run in reverse – replenishing the top reservoir with water from Loch Awe.

HOLLOW MOUNTAIN ➥ 3 miles W of Lochawe on A85 Inverlochy–Oban road.

IONA A boat-shaped mound called Port na Curaich is said to mark the spot where St Columba buried his skin-covered coracle when he arrived from Ireland in 563. Despite the summer visitors, time has stood still during the intervening years in this idyllic bay on Iona's southern shore, preserving the island's allure as a place of solitude and refuge. Elsewhere on Iona, the restored medieval abbey, surrounded by old ruins, Celtic crosses and the unmarked graves of Scottish kings, encourages a more communal experience of sanctity.

MEIKLEOUR BEECH HEDGE In the autumn of 1745 Robert Murray Nairne, laird of Meikleour, had just finished planting a 530m (580yd) long beech hedge when he was swept up in the Jacobite uprising. He died at Culloden fighting for Bonnie Prince Charlie, but his saplings thrived. They are now around 30m (100ft) high and ensure that his descendants enjoy ample privacy. Once every ten years a team of four men using a hydraulic platform give the hedge a shapely trim, a job that occupies them for six weeks.

ROTHIEMURCHUS FOREST The landscape around the shores of Loch an Eilean has hardly altered in 8,000 years. Gnarled Scots pines, with an undergrowth of heather, juniper and bilberry, are remnants of the great Caledonian Forest that

IONA ➡ 1 mile off SW tip of island of Mull. Ferry all year from Fionnphort, Mull.
MEIKLEOUR BEECH HEDGE ➡ Meikleour, 12 miles N of Perth on A93.
ROTHIEMURCHUS FOREST ➡ 5 miles S of Aviemore, signposted off B970.

covered much of north Scotland after the last Ice Age and was gradually destroyed by man's demands for timber, fuel and grazing land. This surviving enclave in the Cairngorms National Park was replanted and preserved over the centuries. It remains a rare and precious habitat for red squirrels, pine martens and some of Scotland's last remaining wild cats, which inhabit rocky outcrops by the loch.

SCOTTISH CRANNOG CENTRE In a large, dimly lit roundhouse, wisps of smoke swirl up from the hearth
towards the high thatched roof. Underfoot, through layers of straw and timber, the loch waters lap against wooden piles. Close by, and safe from thieves or predators on shore, are wicker pens for livestock, a loom, a quern (a hand mill for grinding corn), crude pottery and wooden implements, with a few precious tools of iron.

This is life on a *crannog*, an Iron Age lake dwelling. One has been reconstructed at Loch Tay in Perthshire, based on remains found just across the water. It is an attempt to re-create a prehistoric home and to rediscover ancient skills. Within this strangely comforting place, you feel close to the world 2,000 years ago.

SCOTTISH CRANNOG CENTRE ▶ Off A827, 8 miles W of Aberfeldy.

SCOTLAND

Fife & Southeast Scotland

FALKIRK WHEEL Spectacular in scale, thrilling in design and hypnotic in its steady motion, the world's first rotating boat lift, built in 2001, raises eight boats at a time from an 18th-century canal to a 21st-century aqueduct 33m (108ft) above. Plans to reopen the inland waterways that linked Edinburgh to Glasgow faced a major challenge: the difference in levels between the Forth & Clyde and the Union canals. The giant wheel of steel and concrete provided the solution.

FORTH RAIL BRIDGE Best seen from the waterfront at South Queensferry, the mile-long bridge over the Firth of Forth, completed in 1890, is a celebration of the 19th century's faith in industry and science. Its double-cantilevered spans make no attempt to blend with the environment. The web of tubes and girders rejoices in its muscular development and strength, proclaiming that the railway is striding over water as it takes the march of progress to the North. Contrast this approach with the delicate appearance of the 1964 suspension road bridge, half a mile upstream. Each bridge is a work of art, expressive of its age.

FALKIRK WHEEL ➡ 2 miles W of Falkirk.
FORTH RAIL BRIDGE ➡ A90 at South Queensferry.

MANDERSTON When Sir James Miller married Eveline Curzon,

the daughter of Lord Scarsdale and sister of the Viceroy of India, in 1893, wealth was matched with aristocracy. It was largely to impress her family and friends that Sir James decided to transform his relatively modest 18th-century home into Scotland's grandest country house.

'Money is of no importance whatsoever,' Sir James told the architect of Manderston, John Kinross, when work began in 1901. Reflecting this contempt for cost, the house is mind-boggling in its opulence. The staircase is made of silver; floors and columns are constructed from rare marble. Walls are hung with silk, pelmets coated in gold leaf. It could all be hideously vulgar, but the patina of age has burnished glitter into elegance and the quality of workmanship is so superb that the extravagance becomes a celebration of neoclassical design. Opulence extends beyond the reception rooms and apartments. The barrel–vaulted stables contain teak stalls, brass and marble fittings and tiled troughs. Lady Miller and her friends would occasionally play at being dairymaids in the 22ha (54 acre) gardens, making butter in a marble dairy modelled on medieval cloisters.

ROSSLYN CHAPEL Set above a wooded gorge with a ruined clifftop castle,

the chapel, completed in 1490, is a place of supernatural secrets, coded messages and pagan symbols. The interior is almost overwhelming, for

MANDERSTON ▶ 2 miles E of Duns on A6105.
ROSSLYN CHAPEL ▶ 8 miles S of Edinburgh off A701
Penicuik road.

every column, arch and vault has been richly carved with marvellous designs. Along with the expected saints and angels, there are devils, monsters, green men, dancers, musicians, geometric patterns and Masonic symbols. Among many oddities, avarice is illustrated as a virtue, and there are carvings of cobs of maize, made before Columbus sailed to the New World. The Holy Grail is said to lie concealed in the vaults, guarded by Crusader knights.

SCOTLAND'S SECRET BUNKER

The Soviet bombers can be seen approaching on the radar screens and their likely targets have been plotted on a map. The Tannoy calls for the secretary of state to come down to the Ops Room as clocks tick off the final minutes before nuclear annihilation.

This nightmare from the Cold War is brought to life with chilling conviction in a bunker, hidden deep beneath a field in the Fife countryside near St Andrews. It was designed to be a regional government headquarters in the event of an atomic war. The base was decommissioned in 1992, but its maze of concrete corridors, dormitories, communications rooms and offices remains a sinister and intriguing reminder of the nuclear fear that once gripped Britain.

SCOTLAND'S SECRET BUNKER ▶ 7 miles SE of St Andrews off B9131.

North Highlands & Islands

CALANAIS STANDING STONES Dozens of megaliths, some as tall as 5.5m (18ft), are arranged in a cross with a circle of 13 stones at its centre. At the heart of the circle is a small tomb dating from about 2700 BC. When the Calanais Standing Stones (HS) were erected and for what purpose remain mysteries. Experts suggest that they may be spaced out in megalithic yards, a unit of measurement used throughout Neolithic Britain – but that sheds no light on the enigma. When you visit, reserve your attention for the sheer drama of this far-northern Stonehenge overlooking a sea loch.

CORRIESHALLOCH GORGE The footbridge sways gently underfoot as you cross Corrieshalloch Gorge (NTS). No less a figure than Sir John Fowler, joint designer of the Forth Railway Bridge, built the suspension bridge over the 61m (200ft) deep canyon in 1867. To one side are the Falls of Measach. To the other there is a chasm with ferns and mosses growing from dripping granite walls. Far below lies a world of rare plants created just after the last Ice Age, which has remained inviolate ever since.

CALANAIS STANDING STONES ⏩ 12 miles W of Stornoway off A858, Isle of Lewis.
CORRIESHALLOCH GORGE ⏩ 12 miles S of Ullapool off A835.

EILEAN DONAN CASTLE **Superbly situated on a rocky islet at a point where three deep sea lochs meet,** the seat of the Macraes appears unaltered by the centuries. But Eilean Donan's extraordinary secret is its youth. The 13th-century castle was reduced to utter ruin after a Jacobite uprising in 1719. It was rebuilt as a private home between 1912 and 1932 by John MacRae-Gilstrap, a wealthy descendant of the clan. Farquhar MacRae, his clerk of works, claimed to be guided by visionary dreams as he re-created its medieval halls, passages and turrets without any records to refer to or experts to advise him. When old plans were discovered in a vault in Edinburgh, the accuracy of his second sight was confirmed. Historic character and detail blend with the sophisticated needs of a prewar millionaire, and his dream castle became one of the 20th century's most romantic homes.

JARLSHOF **A complex tapestry of grassy mounds, walls, doors, hearths and passageways** is woven into the landscape at Sumburgh Head in Shetland. The buildings span some 4,000 years and were constructed by many different tribes and races, each one with its own idea of what a home should be. The oldest houses to survive at Jarlshof (HS) belonged to Neolithic farmers in the 3rd millennium BC, who lived within a midden of discarded rubbish that may have been a symbol of ancestral ownership. By the Iron Age,

EILEAN DONAN CASTLE ➡ 10 miles E of Kyle of Lochalsh on A87.
JARLSHOF ➡ 22 miles S of Lerwick, Shetland Islands.

2,000 years later, houses had become more spacious and many were equipped with souterrains: underground passages that may have been used for storing cheese and butter. The next building to appear was the defensive *broch*, a round dry-stone tower dating from the 1st century BC.

Later, the Picts built wheelhouses with chambers radiating from a central hearth. They, in turn, were displaced by Vikings, whose village flourished for 400 years. Finally, Scots warlords built a series of great mansions, the last of which remained inhabited until the 17th century.

WEST HIGHLAND LINE The railway line between Fort William and Mallaig is one of the most scenic in Britain,

with many of its finest views from the viaducts that carry it across glens and rivers. Built between 1897 and 1901 by 'Concrete Bob' McAlpine, founder of the large construction company, they were innovative structures, using hollow concrete piers rather than solid masonry. While the Borrodale Viaduct, near Arisaig, was being built, a horse and cart plummeted 25m (82ft) into an open pier and remains there to this day – an enigma that may puzzle archaeologists in the distant future. The most impressive feature on the line is the 380m (1,247ft) long Glenfinnan Viaduct.

WEST HIGHLAND LINE ▶▶ Fort William to Mallaig.

SCOTLAND

Southwest Scotland

BURRELL COLLECTION Sir William Burrell bequeathed an astonishing collection of 8,000 treasures to the people of Glasgow in 1944. Given their priceless value now, it is also remarkable that he never paid more than £14,500 for any of the items. The museum, built to display the bequest in 1983, has high glass walls that allow light to flood in against the lush green backdrop of the Pollok Country Park beyond.

The breathtaking range of exhibits embraces ancient Egyptian relics, Chinese jade and bronzes, Turkish carpets, arms and armour, silver, glass and 600 paintings, including works by Degas, Bellini, Rembrandt and Raeburn. An integral part of the museum's structure are the monumental porches and arches Burrell bought from the William Randolph Hearst Collection. Burrell stipulated that exhibits must never be loaned out, so make the most of a visit.

CITY CHAMBERS The politicians of the second city of the British Empire certainly knew how to celebrate their importance. Ten million bricks went into the construction of Glasgow's City Chambers. Scottish granite and Italian marble, alabaster, glass and mosaics were lavished on this Renaissance-style palace, which is still the city council's headquarters. The

BURRELL COLLECTION ➡ 2060 Pollokshaws Road, 3 miles S of Glasgow city centre.
CITY CHAMBERS ➡ George Square, Glasgow city centre.

building, designed by the Glasgow-trained William Young and opened by Queen Victoria in 1888, is grand in every respect. The spectacular Carrara marble staircase is the only three-storey example in Europe. In the Council Chamber a stained-glass dome rises to 9m (30ft) and the walls are lined in Spanish mahogany. In the 34m (112ft) long Banqueting Hall, huge murals represent the city's history.

DUMFRIES HOUSE On first approaching Dumfries House, the imposing Palladian exterior appears austere

with little to hint at its ornately decorated interior. Add to this a unique collection of 18th-century rococo furniture and you have one of the most architecturally significant country houses in the United Kingdom. Designed and built by John and Robert Adam in the 1750s, it houses an intact collection of items commissioned from Chippendale: from exotically styled four-poster beds to chamber-pot cupboards.

Built for the 5th Earl of Dumfries, it stayed in private hands until 2007 when it was sold to a consortium of government and heritage organisations, led by the Prince of Wales, with the aim of keeping the house and contents together and opening the property to all.

DUMFRIES HOUSE ▶▶ 1 mile W of Cumnock on A70.

ELECTRIC BRAE The mind plays tricks on those travelling along the Ayrshire coast on the A719 north of Girvan. You can stop the car, leave the brake off and very slowly your vehicle will appear to roll uphill. For a quarter of a mile from the bend overlooking Croy railway viaduct to the west, at 87m (285ft) above sea level, to the wooded Craigencroy Glen to the east, 92m (302ft) above sea level, the configuration on either side of the road makes it look as if the slope is going the other way. It was once believed that this illusion was caused by magnetic attraction, hence the name Electric Brae.

THE ARMADILLO If you stand on the Kingston Bridge crossing over the River Clyde, it is easy to see how the silver shell-like Clyde Auditorium – clad in shiny, reflective 'scales' of aluminium – got its nickname. The building, opened in 1997, has become a landmark to rival Sydney's Opera House.

THE WHANGIE Local legend proclaims that The Whangie came about when the devil whipped his tail across Auchineden Hill. The result was a great gash through the hill. A more prosaic explanation is that the fault occurred through glacial movement in the Ice Age. From the car park, a path leads directly to the summit, from which there are expansive views of Loch Lomond, Ben Lomond, the Kilpatrick Hills and Burncrooks Reservoir.

ELECTRIC BRAE ▶▶ 4 miles S of Dunure on A719.
THE ARMADILLO ▶▶ Finnieston Quay, 1 mile W of Glasgow city centre.
THE WHANGIE ▶▶ 8 miles N of Glasgow. 4 mile walk from Queen's View car park on A809 NW of Carbeth.

A landmark that rivals Sydney's opera house

Index

UVW

Picture Credits

Acknowledgements

For Toucan Books
Editors Jane Hutchings,
Andrew Kerr-Jarrett
Art Editor Nick Avery
Picture Research Sharon Southren,
Mia Stewart-Wilson, Christine Vincent
Proofreader Marion Dent
Indexer Michael Dent

For Reader's Digest Books
Editorial Director Julian Browne
Art Director Anne-Marie Bulat
Managing Editor Nina Hathway
Project Editor Rachel Weaver
Project Art Editor Julie Bennett
Picture Resource Manager
Sarah Stewart-Richardson
Pre-press Technical Manager
Dean Russell
Senior Production Controller
Katherine Tibbals

Origination by ImageScanhouse

Printed and bound in China

Front cover Stonehenge, Wiltshire.
Back cover Angel of the North, Tyneside.
Page 1 Eden Project, Cornwall.
Pages 2–3 Clifton Suspension Bridge,
Somerset. **Pages 4–5** Eilean Donan
Castle, Scotland. **Page 6** London Eye
and Big Ben. **Pages 8–9** Croyde Bay,
Cornwall. **Pages 24–25** Windsor Castle,
Berkshire. **Pages 58–59** View from
Victoria Tower, Houses of Parliament.
Pages 70–71 Lavender field, Norfolk.
Pages 84–85 Peak District, Derbyshire.
Pages 124–125 Lake District, Cumbria.
Pages 140–141 Rookhope Burn, Durham.
Pages 154–155 Mount Snowdon, Wales.
Pages 166–167 Iona Abbey, Scotland.

We are committed both to the quality
of our products and the service we
provide to our customers. We value your
comments, so please do contact us on
08705 113366 or via our website at
www.readersdigest.co.uk

If you have any comments or suggestions
about the contents of our books, email us at
gbeditorial@readersdigest.co.uk

ISBN 978 0 276 44572 9
Book Code 400-479 UP0000-1
Oracle Code 250014572S.00.24